Unlikely Heroines

Recent Titles in
Contributions in Women's Studies

Radiant Daughters: Fictional American Women
Thelma J. Shinn

New World, New Roles: A Documentary History of Women in Pre-Industrial America
Sylvia R. Frey and Marian J. Morton

Gender, Ideology, and Action: Historical Perspectives on Women's Public Lives
Janet Sharistanian, editor

American Women and Political Participation: Impacts of Work, Generation, and Feminism
Karen Beckwith

The American Victorian Woman: The Myth and the Reality
Mabel Collins Donnelly

Gender and Destiny: Women Writers and the Holocaust
Marlene E. Heinemann

Nineteenth-Century Women Writers of the English-Speaking World
Rhoda B. Nathan, editor

Women's Rights in France
Dorothy McBride Stetson

Charity, Challenge, and Change: Religious Dimensions of the Mid-Nineteenth Century Women's Movement in Germany
Catherine M. Prelinger

Woman as Mediatrix: Essays on Nineteenth-Century European Women Writers
Avriel H. Goldberger, editor

Women and American Foreign Policy: Lobbyists, Critics, and Insiders
Edward P. Crapol, editor

From Ladies to Women: The Organized Struggle for Woman's Rights in the Reconstruction Era
Israel Kugler

UNLIKELY HEROINES

Nineteenth-Century
American Women Writers
and the Woman Question

Ann R. Shapiro

Contributions in Women's Studies, Number 81

GREENWOOD PRESS
New York · Westport, Connecticut · London

Library of Congress Cataloging-in-Publication Data

Shapiro, Ann R., 1937–
  Unlikely heroines.

  (Contributions in women's studies, ISSN 0147-104X ;
no. 81)
  Bibliography: p.
  Includes index.
  1. American fiction—19th century—History and
criticism.   2. American fiction—Women authors—History
and criticism.   3. Feminism in literature.   4. Women
in literature.   5. Heroines in literature.   6. Women
and literature—United States.   7. Feminism and
literature—United States.   I. Title.   II. Series.
  PS374.F45S48   1987   813'.4'099287   86-22750
  ISBN 0-313-25422-2 (lib. bdg. : alk. paper)

Library of Congress Catalog Card Number: 86-22750
ISBN: 0-313-25422-2
ISSN: 0147-104X

First published in 1987

Greenwood Press, Inc.
88 Post Road West, Westport, Connecticut 06881

Printed in the United States of America

∞

The paper used in this book complies with the
Permanent Paper Standard issued by the National
Information Standards Organization (Z39.48-1984).

10 9 8 7 6 5 4 3 2 1

TO MY CHILDREN
Rona, Wendy, and Edward

Contents

Acknowledgments

I want to thank Joy Gould Boyum, who provided both the challenge and support I needed in developing the early stages of the manuscript. I am also grateful to James W. Tuttleton for his helpful suggestions.

In addition, credit should go to Michael Vinciguerra and Robert Mark at the State University of New York at Farmingdale for giving me the time I needed to complete the manuscript.

And finally, special thanks are due my mother, Jeanette Rabinowitz, and the friends whose encouragement was invaluable: Michael Sillerman, Sondra Melzer, Eve Stwertka, Virginia Fairweather, Alice and Sol Tennenbaum, Carolyn and Christopher Ballaban.

Unlikely Heroines

Introduction

American literature, we have long been told, is about heroes who leave civilization and domesticity to forge their own destinies, independent of social constraints. Huck Finn lights out for the territory, Ishmael boards a whaling ship, and Natty Bumpo triumphs in the wilderness. Such heroes embody Emerson's vision of self-reliance and Thoreau's notion of a man marching to a different drummer. This is a view of classical American literature which has been propounded by such leading scholars as Vernon L. Parrington, F. O. Matthiessen, and, more recently, Leslie Fiedler, George Stade, and Martin Green. Such an analysis is certainly supportable if American literature, especially of the nineteenth century, is limited to works by and about men.

The fact is, however, that much of the fiction of the nineteenth century was written by and about women. Hawthorne understandably decried "that d——d mob of scribbling women," whose novels outsold his own. Most of these "scribbling women" are little known today, but at least one, Harriet Beecher Stowe, became America's most widely read novelist. Yet Matthiessen could find no place for Stowe in the period he called the "American Renaissance," and Leslie Fiedler would later write that American literature turns "from society to nature to avoid the facts of wooing, marriage and childbearing."[1] But wooing, marriage, childbearing, and also childrearing are some of the very concerns that occupied Stowe and most of the women writers of her time.

As various critics have recently observed, there seems to be an underlying assumption that American literature has been exclusively male, while women's literature is something else, presumably unworthy of the designation "literature."[2] According to George Stade, for example, fiction by nineteenth-century American women was "sentimental, narcissistic, domestic, diffusely religious and female chauvinistic."[3] Stade does not enlighten us by naming any works to which these adjectives may be applied, so that we are obliged to look for the works, read them, and make our own judgments.

The first problem, of course, is what to read. While recent college literature anthologies include occasional short pieces by women writers, no woman novelist of the period has a secure place in the canon. Also, feminist critics in recent years have been making nineteenth-century fiction by long-neglected women writers accessible through publishing new editions of out-of-print books, but it is too early for a consensus on which writers or which specific works demand inclusion with Cooper, Hawthorne, Melville, Twain, and the other luminaries in the American pantheon.

In the absence of any consensus on the most important women writers of the period, a selection of six novels was made here on the basis of both quality and content. All six novels were written in the last half of the century, and the authors were considered outstanding for their time by critics of nineteenth- or twentieth-century American literature. In addition, each deals with an issue that surfaces repeatedly in women's fiction—namely, the "Woman Question," a term often used in the nineteenth century in the ongoing debate about woman's role.

Harriet Beecher Stowe's *Uncle Tom's Cabin* was not only the outstanding best seller of its time and widely praised by critics, but its feminism has been intermittently recognized since its publication. Moreover, Stowe's conception of slavery as a woman's issue was typical insofar as the women's movement grew out of abolition.

Although Louisa May Alcott ranked among the most popular writers of the period, it is only recently that she has been viewed as a literary artist and feminist. While critics agree that *Little Women* was her best book, *Work* was included because of its more explicit exploration of some critical aspects of the Woman Question, involving work options for women and difficulties of resolving the conflicting needs of affiliation and independence.

Elizabeth Stuart Phelps, Mary Wilkins Freeman, and Sarah Orne Jewett generally have been well regarded in the development of realism and local color. Little has been written about the Woman Question in the works of Freeman and Jewett. Critics concur that *Pembroke* is the best of Freeman's novels. It is of interest in this study because it attempts to resolve the Woman Question by creating a matriarchal society, a characteristic solution of several novels of the nineteenth and early twentieth centuries.[4] As for Sarah Orne Jewett, there is critical agreement that *The Country of the Pointed Firs* is her masterpiece, but *A Country Doctor* was selected because of its detailed argument on a woman's choice between marriage and a career as a physician. Early criticism ignored Phelps's concern with the Woman Question; however, in recent years feminist critics have attempted to revive interest in *The Story of Avis* and *The Silent Partner* as exemplary works about women. *The Silent Partner* was chosen because woman's involvement in the factory system is vital to an understanding of her perceived role at the time.

Finally, Kate Chopin's *The Awakening* has recently been reconsidered as an important work of a forgotten writer who courageously confronted social and sexual aspects of the Woman Question. It is unique in American fiction of the period in suggesting that a free woman had to reject all social constraints, including her marriage.

There is no claim that the novels discussed here are definitive examples of the fiction produced by nineteenth-century American women. Many others were reviewed, but in order to allow for depth of analysis the selections were limited to six. The present work is intended to add to the understanding of a literature which, as the critical history of each novel presented in the following chapters reveals, has often been bypassed and at times poorly understood.

Consideration of the novels in the context of the issues that concerned the authors and informed the work is intended to reveal new aspects of individual works. Moreover, the novels taken together present a thematic unity, which will be explored in the conclusion of this work.

The heroines of these novels are called "unlikely" because on the surface they do not appear to be heroic in the classic sense. They are slave women and housemaids, rural matriarchs and dissatisfied wives, factory workers and middle-class professionals. But if they are different from the heroes of American literature, they are also surprisingly similar. They do not hunt whales or raft on the Mississippi, but they exhibit the same urge to break with tradition, the same rejection of conventional values, and the same desire for adventure.

NOTES

1. Leslie Fiedler, *Love and Death in the American Novel* (New York: Stein & Day, 1966), p. 25.

2. See, for example, Judith Fetterley, *The Resisting Reader: A Feminist Approach to American Fiction* (Bloomington: Indiana University Press, 1978); and Paul Lauter, ed., *Reconstructing American Literature: Courses, Syllabi, Issues* (Old Westbury, N.Y.: Feminist Press, 1983).

3. George Stade, "Men, Boys and Wimps," *New York Times Book Review*, August 12, 1984, p. 22.

4. See, for example, Louisa May Alcott, *Little Women* (New York: Modern Library, 1983); Sarah Orne Jewett, *The Country of the Pointed Firs* in *Short Fiction of Sarah Orne Jewett and Mary Freeman*, ed. Barbara H. Solomon (New York: New American Library, 1979), pp. 47–51; or Charlotte Perkins Gilman, *Herland* (New York: Pantheon, 1979).

1

The Woman Question

By the middle of the nineteenth century, articles on the Woman Question filled the journals. Everyone, it seemed, had something to say about woman's role, woman's work, woman's rights, and woman's destiny. More than 100 years ago, Elizabeth Cady Stanton, Susan B. Anthony, and a host of others were stirring up arguments that were no less far reaching than those advanced by Betty Friedan and Gloria Steinem, today.

Why the interest in the Woman Question surfaced is difficult to explain with certainty, but historians offer a variety of explanations. The women's rights movement has been called an offshoot of abolition, a cause involving many women, who ultimately identified their own situation with that of the slaves.[1] Another explanation is that women belatedly were responding to the liberal ideals of the French and American Revolutions.[2] But historian William L. O'Neill suggests that the most important cause for the rise of feminism in the 1830s was the development of the conjugal family system. O'Neill's point is that prior to the nineteenth century, the family was not an isolated unit: the home in town was frequently a shop as well as a domicile; and the farmhouse was an integral part of the working world. But with the rise of commerce and industry, work was gradually removed from the home, thus creating a separation between mothers and children on the one hand, and the working world on the other. Thus women who desired independence and equality found themselves relegated to a domestic world from which it was difficult to escape.[3]

The "oppressive domesticity" in the nineteenth century of which O'Neill writes became apparent in the glorification of the so-called "True Woman," an ideal of virtuous feminity which was increasingly threatened by the emerging "New Woman."[4] While the argument for women's rights was pressed not only by reformers but eventually by leading editors of some of the more prestigious periodicals,[5] the prevailing view continued to glorify True Womanhood. Women were exhorted to devote themselves to a "right understanding and faithful and cheerful performance of social and family duties," to be conscious of their "inferiority" and to "reverence" the wishes of their husbands. Historian Barbara Welter sums up "the attributes of True Womanhood" as "piety, purity, submissiveness and domesticity."[6] Marriage was expected to be a woman's whole life, and while many women cheerfully accepted their lot, women's rights advocates argued that women's growth was being stultified.

One of the earliest writers to comment on the Woman Question was Harriet Martineau, who after her visit to America in 1837 lamented, "The Americans have, in the treatment of women fallen below, not only their own democratic principles, but the practice of some parts of the Old World."[7] She lamented that women were excluded from philosophy, science, and literature so that all that remained to them was marriage. Martineau anticipated the argument that would be raised by reformers in the early years of the movement when she asked how the restrictions imposed upon women could be reconciled with the principles of the Declaration of Independence in its insistence upon "inalienable rights."

Only one year later Sarah Grimké published *Letters on the Equality of the Sexes and the Condition of Women* (1838), which has been called "the first major work by an American feminist."[8] In the *Letters* Grimké took to task the Protestant ministry for perpetuating the notion that the Bible sanctions woman's dependency on man. Like Martineau, she felt that American women were victimized by an overemphasis on marriage, which prevented them from realizing their full potential. She observed that since marriage was supposed to be the "*sine qua non* of happiness and human existence," girls were poorly educated and encouraged to be fashionable, mere "pretty toys" and "instruments of pleasure."[9]

Margaret Fuller (1845) expanded Grimké's argument when she suggested that in marriage, women, like slaves, often seemed little more than man's property. Without denying the primacy of woman's role as mother, Fuller nonetheless insisted that woman's sphere could not be limited to the mother role. Instead, she argued for women to have freedom to develop both mind and body so that they would be fit for life's challenges.[10]

The notion that women, like slaves, were being denied fundamental rights was given official statement in the Declaration of Sentiments and Resolutions issued at the Seneca Falls Convention in 1848. Historians typically date the inception of the women's movement from this historical event.[11] Called by Lucretia Mott, Martha C. Wright, Elizabeth Cady Stanton, and Mary Ann McClintock in order to discuss what they termed in their notice of the convention "the social, civil and religious condition and rights of woman," Seneca Falls was the first of many conventions where women gathered expressly to demand rights which they felt had been unjustly denied them. The Seneca Falls Declaration was a paraphrase of the Declaration of Independence in which the rights of woman were asserted as part of the rights of humankind. The tyrant identified in the Declaration of Sentiments was not King George but man, and all laws which conflicted "with the true and substantial happiness of woman" were declared of "no validity."[12]

While the major thrust of the Declaration of Sentiments was for political equality, Elizabeth Cady Stanton made it clear that it was also meant to draw attention to the inequities perpetuated by woman's role in other spheres. Explaining how she came to initiate the Seneca Falls Convention, Stanton wrote of her discontent with "woman's position as wife, mother, housekeeper, physician, and spiritual guide." She lamented "the wearied anxious look of the majority of women," and spurred by her own observations of "oppression" and her readings on the legal status of women, she concluded that it was necessary to hold what she called "a public meeting for protest and discussion."[13]

The Seneca Falls Declaration called for the franchise, for improved educational opportunity, for admission of women to the ministry. It spoke of property rights and the civil death of women in marriage; it called for changes in divorce laws, which as then written acknowledged "the supremacy of man." In addition, buried in the long list of grievances was an indictment of man because he had "usurped the prerogative of Jehovah himself, claiming it was his right to assign for her a sphere of action, when that belongs to her conscience and to her God."[14] It was the question of woman's "sphere of action" more than any other which continued to preoccupy Stanton and her generation. Above all they decried what they considered woman's degradation in marriage. In 1853 Elizabeth Cady Stanton wrote to Susan B. Anthony, "The right idea of marriage is at the foundation of all reforms."[15]

During the Civil War years, the Woman Question was partially eclipsed by war issues, but when the war ended, women's rights once again became a compelling cause, touched off by the passage of the Thirteenth and Fourteenth Amendments. Leaders of the women's movement had long identified with the slaves and assumed that recognition of the rights of blacks would also mean recognition of women's rights. But, in fact, the Constitution, as newly amended, would continue to exclude women. Stanton and her cohorts protested:

We have stood with the black man in the Constitution over half a century and it is fitting now that the constitutional door is open that we should enter with him into the political kingdom. . . . Enfranchise him, and we are left outside with lunatics, idiots and criminals for another twenty years.[16]

Suffrage, formerly only a single aspect of the larger women's movement, now seemed a priority. The Fourteenth Amendment introduced the word "male" into the Constitution for the first time and, therefore, according to Eleanor Flexner, "raised the issue of whether women were actually citizens of the United States."[17] While Elizabeth Cady Stanton and Susan B. Anthony fought vigorously against the passage of the Fourteenth Amendment out of fear that its passage would be a severe blow to women's rights, other movement leaders continued to support the amendment because of sympathy for the black man. By 1869 a major schism had formed, and two suffrage organizations were founded, the National Woman

Suffrage Association (under Elizabeth Cady Stanton and Susan B. Anthony) and the American Woman Suffrage Association. The National Woman Suffrage Association continued to press for a variety of reforms affecting women, while the American Suffrage Association concentrated on obtaining the franchise in various states. Despite the increased agitation for suffrage, articles by advocates of women's rights revealed that for most, suffrage was regarded as a means, not an end, the real end being woman's equal participation in society. And this goal often united suffragists and anti-suffragists alike.

A common concern of all was opportunity in the job market, and some of the issues raised seem remarkably modern. Antoinette Brown Blackwell (1873), for example, insisted that work was necessary not only to provide financial support but also to provide self-fulfillment. While she acknowledged that "the paramount social duties of women are household duties," she insisted that "every woman, rich or poor, not actually an invalid confined to one room is in imperative need of a daily distinct change of thought and employment."[18]

Even while the fight for suffrage continued, statements such as this remind us that the issues went far beyond suffrage. In 1870 Laura Bullard reemphasized Elizabeth Cady Stanton's concern about marriage, declaring: "The solemn and profound question of marriage . . . is of more vital consequence to woman's welfare, reaches down to a deeper depth in woman's heart and more thoroughly constitutes the core of the woman's movement than any such superficial and fragmentary question as woman's suffrage."[19] Above all, movement leaders stressed that women needed equality in marriage. Indeed, even the staid Elizabeth Cady Stanton was among those willing to abandon marriage for "free love" as long as women remained disadvantaged in the marriage contract. Stanton declared:

I have worked thirty years for woman's suffrage, and I now feel that suffrage is but the vestibule of woman's emancipation. The men and women who are dabbling with the suffrage movement for women should be at once . . . and emphatically warned that what they mean logically if not consciously in all they say is next social equality and next Freedom or in a word Free Love, and if they wish to get out of the boat, they should for safety get out now, for delays are dangerous.[20]

This view of love as distinct from marriage was developed more fully by the notorious sisters, Tennie C. Claflin and Victoria Woodhull. More outspoken than any of their contemporaries on the question of sexuality, Claflin and Woodhull tried to make clear that they were not advocating "common looseness." Claflin insisted that "*forced love*" was "prostitution."[21] As long as women were obligated to provide sex for their husbands, they were clearly subservient, and such subservience could not be countenanced. As Claflin made clear in her book *Constitutional Equality: A Right of Women* (1871), what was necessary was freedom and equality for women, which involved virtually all aspects of women's lives. And like Stanton and other suffragists, she hoped that the goal could be achieved through suffrage. The "Woman Question," she promised, would "vitalize the party that shall become its champion."[22]

As women's rights advocates became increasingly visible, it is not surprising that the arguments against their cause intensified. These arguments, which began to appear with increased frequency after the Civil War, rarely attempt to deal with the problems raised by reformers. Rather they continue to reflect prejudices about the nature and condition of women. Extremists were ready to blame most of society's ills on women's efforts to expand their role. A typical view was that of Dr. Nathan Allen, who ascribed the decline of New England productivity to a decrease in population caused by "the growth and prevalence of the practice of abortion" and women's "over-development of the brain and over-devotion to intellectual pursuits."[23]

Few, however, went as far as Dr. Allen in outright condemnation of women. The attack against suffrage and equal rights was, in fact, more often couched in chivalrous terms. Francis Parkman, in arguing against suffrage, declared, "everybody knows that the physical and mental constitution of woman is more delicate than in the other sex. . . . " He therefore concluded that men are "made for conflict," while women possess "moral elevation."[24] It is never made clear why this distinction, even if accurate, should prevent women from voting, but the notion that women's innate nature precluded political participation was endemic. Another critic of suffrage wrote in 1869, "Politics, it must be confessed, appear thus far to be prevailingly and stubbornly if not incorrigibly male."[25]

Both suffragists and those who took a stand against enfranchisement for women agreed that the family was in trouble. But where suffragists insisted that the problem would be resolved when women enjoyed greater equality, opponents maintained the opposite. "The conclusive objection to the political enfranchisement of women," Orestes Brownson wrote, "is that it would weaken and finally break up and destroy the Christian family." He therefore concluded, "Woman was created to be a wife and mother; that is her destiny."[26]

The issue was heated, and the rhetoric often suggested more fear than thought. An anonymous writer in *The North American Review* (1880) argued, "the unhappy condition of a part of their [women's] sex" should not be introduced into politics because it would "poison the air with moral typhoid. Other questions of sex, or marriage, divorce and 'free love' would rush in with it."[27] What these anti-suffragist arguments suggest above all is a need to maintain the status quo. The social structure was being threatened, and panic seemed to have set in.

But despite the panic, new issues continued to surface through the last decade of the century. The case against conventional marriage was extended by Elizabeth Cady Stanton's daughter, Harriet Stanton Blatch, to include a plea for voluntary motherhood. In 1891 she declared, "Motherhood is sacred—that is voluntary motherhood; but the woman who bears unwelcome children is outraging every duty she owes the race."[28]

In 1895 Elizabeth Cady Stanton herself once again raised an issue that had been argued earlier by the Grimké sisters, namely that the Bible had been used to keep women in their place. She declared that the Bible was not the word of God but rather the creation of "fallible man." "Whatever the Bible may be made to do in Hebrew or Greek," she wrote, "in plain English, it does not exalt and dignify woman.[29] It is little wonder that the timid recoiled in fear as Stanton repeatedly shook the foundations of society, striking at every icon that seemed to stand in the way of equality for women.

If by the end of the century Stanton was still the prophet of the movement, others were entering the fray, adding their voices to hers as they continued to analyze women's condition. Undoubtedly the most important and innovative statement of the issues in the final decade of the century was Charlotte Perkins Gilman's *Women and Economics* (1898). William L. O'Neill called *Women and Economics* "the most influential book ever written by an American feminist," and Eleanor Flexner added that it was "the single most significant contribution" on the Woman Question.[30]

Gilman above all decried a social system which encouraged men to have careers and develop in the world while it permitted women only to marry. She lamented that while a young man was permitted to use whatever powers he had to succeed in the world, a young woman was limited to whatever advantages could come to her "through a small gold ring."[31] Not only were women frustrated in their desires to grow, but Gilman felt they were also deprived economically because they had to depend on their husbands' work rather than their own. Far from seeing a conflict between woman's sex role and her drive for independence, she felt that women who had a greater sense of individualism would make better wives and mothers. Gilman anticipated many of the arguments of twentieth-century feminists when she insisted that independent work was necessary to every individual regardless of sex. She felt that women deprived of work and left to be female and nothing else were martyrs to an unjust cause.

Like Stanton and other earlier reformers, Gilman attacked the Bible and the religious institutions for keeping women in their place. "As religion developed," Gilman declared, woman's "place receded, until Paul commanded her to be silent in the churches. And she has been silent until to-day."[32]

Gilman's remedy for the social and economic ills inherent in woman's condition seems strikingly modern. Marriage, as she saw it, was not satisfactory because of the division of roles between men and women. She went so far as to advocate that married couples make beds, sweep, and cook together so that they would be "class equals."[33]

Despite the title *Women and Economics*, Gilman's primary concern was social equality, which she saw as a necessary concomitant of women's working. She attributed the improvement in women's lives during her lifetime to their being forced into economic activity. Interestingly, it is in her comments on the fiction of her day that Gilman most clearly expressed her view of what women's lives ought to be:

In the fiction of to-day women are continually taking larger places in the action of the story. They are given personal characteristics beyond those of physical beauty. And they are no longer content simply to *be*: they *do*. They are showing qualities of bravery, endurance, strength, foresight; and power of the swift execution of well-conceived plans.[34]

In the absence of literary criticism by women of the period, this statement is significant in suggesting that women perceived the writing of their contemporaries quite differently from men, who tended to seek moral elevation in women's novels rather than role models.

As the century drew to a close, women had not achieved suffrage, nor had they reformed marriage. But they had succeeded in opening up doors in education and the professions. Eleanor Flexner attributes the failure to attain suffrage to organized opposition from special interest groups such as the liquor lobby and the political machines. In contrast, she suggests that the opposition to women in the professions and in education was "guerilla-like" and "sporadic."[35] Thus, women were able to chalk up gains that eluded them in the political arena.

Disappointed by the failure of suffrage and other reforms, Elizabeth Cady Stanton was still able to look back with pride on a half century of progress. At the International Council of Women in Washington, D.C., in 1888 she noted that only half a century earlier women had been "bond slaves," denied access to education and the trades and professions.[36] While the battle was not over, much had changed.

By 1886 there were 266 colleges for women and 297 mechanical and scientific institutions which accepted women, for a total of 563 institutions enrolling 35,976 female students. These figures are in contrast to 802 institutions of higher education serving 78,185 men.[37] While opportunities in education for women still lagged behind those for men, clearly the gains in a relatively short time were substantial when we consider that at the beginning of the century in most of the country girls were excluded from high school, and higher education for women did not exist at all until Oberlin opened its doors to both sexes in 1833.

Increased educational opportunity did not always translate into increased economic opportunity, but progress was also made in women's employment. Because of rapid industrial growth in the late nineteenth century, women workers were in rising demand. The number of women workers grew from 2,647,000 gainfully em-

ployed in 1880 to 4,005,500 ten years later, from 15.2 to 17.2 percent of the total work force.[38] Nonetheless, women still filled the
lowest-paying jobs, and it remained for them to organize into unions
to secure higher pay and better working conditions.

The last decade of the century saw more professions open to
women, but progress was slow. In 1849 Elizabeth Blackwell made
history as the first woman graduate of an American medical school,
and by 1886 there were 390 women practicing medicine in twenty-
six states.[39]

Entering the legal profession was even more problematic because
licenses were granted by the Supreme Court of each state. While
some states were willing to license women lawyers, others reacted
with panic to female applicants. The decision rendered by the Illinois Supreme Court in 1870 in response to Mrs. Myra Bradwell's
application for a law license is representative of an attitude that
prevailed in some parts of the country:

That God designed the sexes to occupy different spheres of action, that it
belonged to men to make, apply and execute the laws, was regarded as an
almost axiomatic truth. . . . We are certainly warranted in saying that
when the Legislature gave to this court the power of granting licenses to
practice law, it was not with the slightest expectation that this privilege
would be extended equally to men and women.[40]

If women were excluded from the law in some states, they,
nonetheless, could become ministers and professors as well as sci-
entists and architects. But their numbers were minimal, and obstacles were placed in their way so that only the most determined
succeeded. By the end of the century women were represented
mainly in low-paying nonprofessional jobs.

It would take the better part of the twentieth century for them
to realize most of the gains their sisters had envisioned 100 years
earlier. And it is because of these gains that we can listen to the
voices of the nineteenth century with renewed interest and understanding. The chords that the leaders of the women's movement
struck are still reverberating. We can only regret that they did not
live to see their dreams realized.

NOTES

1. Page Smith, *Daughters of the Promised Land* (Boston: Little, Brown, 1970), p. 104.

2. William L. O'Neill, *Everyone Was Brave* (Chicago: Quadrangle, 1969), p. 3.

3. Ibid., pp. 4–6.

4. See, for example, Harriet Beecher Stowe, "What Will You Do with Her? Or, the Woman Question," in *Household Papers and Stories* (Boston: Houghton Mifflin, 1896), pp. 231–48.

5. E. L. Godkin, Thomas Wentworth Higginson, and William Dean Howells all supported aspects of the feminist position. See particularly E. L. Godkin's articles on the Woman Question in the *Nation*, 1867–1870.

6. Barbara Welter, "The Cult of True Womanhood: 1829–1860," *American Quarterly* 18 (Summer 1966): 151–74, rpt. in *Our American Sisters: Women in American Life and Thought*, ed. Jean E. Friedman and William G. Shade (Boston: Allyn and Bacon, 1973), pp. 103–5, 115.

7. Harriet Martineau, *Society in America*, Vol. 2 (New York: Saunders & Otley, 1837), p. 226.

8. O'Neill, *Everyone Was Brave*, p. 11.

9. Sarah Grimké, *Letters on the Equality of the Sexes and the Condition of Women* (Boston, 1838), pp. 14–121, rpt. in *The Feminist Papers*, ed. Alice S. Rossi (New York: Bantam, 1974), p. 312.

10. Margaret Fuller, *Woman in the Nineteenth Century* (1845; rpt. New York: Norton, 1971), p. 176.

11. See, for example, Mary R. Beard, *Woman as Force in History* (New York: Macmillan, 1947), p. 114; and Eleanor Flexner, *Century of Struggle*, rev. ed. (Cambridge: Belknap-Harvard University Press, 1975), p. 71.

12. Document 5 (I:67–74), Seneca Falls Convention, Seneca Falls, New York, July 19–20, 1848, including the Declaration of Sentiments and Resolutions, rpt. in *The Concise History of Woman Suffrage*, ed. Mari Jo Buhle and Paul Buhle (Urbana: University of Illinois, 1978), pp. 94–96.

13. Theodore Stanton and Harriet Stanton Blatch, eds., *Elizabeth Cady Stanton* (New York: Arno, 1969), pp. 144–45.

14. Buhle and Buhle, *Concise History*, p. 95.

15. Elizabeth Cady Stanton, Letter to Susan B. Anthony, March 1, 1853, in Nelson Manfred Black, *The Road to Reno* (New York: Macmillan, 1962), p. 88.

16. As quoted in O'Neill, *Everyone Was Brave*, p. 17.

17. Flexner, *Century of Struggle*, p. 146.

18. Antoinette Brown Blackwell, "Relation of Woman's Work in the Household to the Work Outside," in *Papers and Letters Presented at the First*

Woman's Congress of the Association for the Advancement of Woman, New York, October 1873 (New York, 1874), pp. 178–84, rpt. in Aileen S. Kraditor, *Up from the Pedestal* (New York: Quadrangle, 1968), p. 153.

19. Laura Bullard, "What Flag Shall We Fly?" *Revolution* 27 (October, 1870): 264.

20. Elizabeth Cady Stanton, *Newark Call*, as quoted in Smith, *Daughters*, p. 152.

21. Tennie C. Claflin, *Constitutional Equality: A Right of Women*, p. 75, as quoted in Smith, *Daughters*, p. 151.

22. Claflin, as quoted in Smith, *Daughters*, p. 71.

23. Nathan Allen, "The Other Side of the Question," *Nation* 5 (1867); 316.

24. Francis Parkman, "The Woman Question," *North American Review* 129 (1879): 304–8.

25. "Is There Such a Thing as Sex?" *Nation* 8 (1869): 87–88.

26. Orestes A. Brownson, the Woman Question (1869 and 1873)," in Kraditor, *Up from the Pedestal*, pp. 192–93.

27. "The Woman Question Again," *North American Review* 130 (1880): 25–26.

28. Harriet Stanton Blatch, "Voluntary Motherhood (1891)," in Kraditor, *Up from the Pedestal*, p. 169.

29. Elizabeth Cady Stanton, ed., *The Woman's Bible* (New York: European Publishing, 1895), Part 1, pp. 7–13, rpt, in Rossi, *Feminist Papers*, p. 406.

30. O'Neill, *Everyone Was Brave*, p. 131; Flexner, *Century of Struggle*, p. 239.

31. Charlotte Perkins Gilman, *Women and Economics*, ed. Carl L. Degler (1898; rpt. New York: Harper, 1966), p. 71.

32. Ibid., p. 219.

33. Ibid., p. 219.

34. Ibid., p. 150.

35. Flexner, *Century of Struggle*, p. 305.

36. See Smith, *Daughters*, p. 259.

37. Ibid., p. 196.

38. Flexner, *Century of Struggle*, p. 197.

39. Smith, *Daughters*, pp. 278–79.

40. Elizabeth Cady Stanton, Susan Anthony, and Mathilda Joslyn Gage, eds., *The History of Woman Suffrage*, Vol. 2 (Rochester, N.Y., 1881) pp. 611–12, as quoted in Flexner, *Century of Struggle*, p. 122.

2

Motherhood, the True Woman, and the New Woman: Harriet Beecher Stowe, *Uncle Tom's Cabin* (1852)

Harriet Beecher Stowe was born in 1811 in Litchfield, Connecticut. Her mother died when she was only four, a trauma which probably accounts for her idealization of mothers in much of her fiction. Her father, Lyman Beecher, was a prominent minister steeped in an orthodox Calvinism, which his daughter would come to reject in adulthood.

Her marriage at age twenty-four to Calvin Stowe, a widowed minister nine years older than she, has been described as something less than romantic.[1] She bore five children in the first seven years of her marriage and then two more, one of whom died in infancy. At the time she wrote *Uncle Tom's Cabin* she is reported to have thought of herself as an overworked housewife,[2] but its great success both here and in Europe changed her life. Although she received a royalty of only 10 percent, she became the principal wage earner of her family, who thereafter lived mainly on earnings from her writing and investments. When she died in 1896 she was famous as both writer and reformer.

Stowe did not participate in the women's rights movement directly, but her writing indicates continued interest in the issues raised by activists. Slavery was for Stowe a woman's issue, which she explored in detail in her two slavery novels, *Uncle Tom's Cabin* and *Dred*. And when slavery finally ended, she continued to pursue the Woman Question in other contexts, particularly in the years 1868–1875. She wrote to George Eliot in 1869, "We are busy now in the next great emancipation—that of woman."[3] Several works written around this time indicate that Stowe was indeed involved with the Woman Question. They are *Lady Byron Vindicated* (1870); the New York novels: *Pink and White Tyranny* (1871), *My Wife and I* (1871), and *We and Our Neighbors* (1875); and a number of stories and articles which were eventually combined in *Household Papers and Stories* (1896).

Although critics have complained about an inconsistency in Stowe's views, some clear patterns emerge.[4] On the issue of work she was unequivocal in her belief that women were disadvantaged and needed greater opportunities. She complained about low pay, poor working conditions, and limitations on the kinds of work available.[5] To rectify inequities, she advocated reforms that sound very much like those sought in recent years by supporters of the Equal Rights Amendment. Specifically she proposed the "right of every woman to receive equal pay with man for work she does equally well," and the "right of any women to any work for which by her natural organization and talent, she is peculiarly adapted."[6]

Stowe's solution was to open up professional careers of all kinds for women. She insisted that women could if they wished be physicians, architects, landscape gardeners, or even "teachers of a naval school," expounding "the mysteries of ocean navigation."[7]

Several of Stowe's novels argue that women who choose leisure over work squander their lives. In *My Wife and I* Ida Van Arsdale complains that the lives of girls between the time they leave school and get married are a "perfect waste."[8] Even after marriage, many women, according to Stowe, were not only a burden to their husbands and families but destructive to themselves and others. Two devastating portraits of such women are Marie St. Claire in *Uncle Tom's Cabin* and Lillie in *Pink and White Tyranny*. Of Marie St. Claire, more will be said later. Lillie is the embodiment of the True Woman described earlier, and Stowe finds little to admire.

Lillie's talents are limited to speaking French with a good accent and writing sentimental notes in a pretty handwriting. While she is outwardly submissive, she soon turns into a petty tyrant who uses a husband to pay her bills. When there is a crisis, she develops a "sick headache," and in time the husband who once adored her falls out of love with the useless creature he has helped create.

For Stowe marriage was sacred, and she was sharply critical of men as well as women who failed to live up to their marital obligations, even advocating a woman's rights to divorce in extreme cases. In *Lady Byron Vindicated* Stowe suggests that the marriage vow should have been dissolved because of the extreme cruelty of Lord Byron, who she alleges attempted to cover up an incestuous relationship with his sister by maligning Lady Byron. Stowe wrote passionately about the Byron case that "man may wallow in filth like the swine, may turn his home into a hell, beat and torture his children, forsake the marriage-bed for four rivals yet all this does *not* dissolve the marriage vow on her part. . . . "[9] In this sustained argument for the rights of women in marriage Stowe reflects the prevailing view of movement leaders.

Nonetheless, she often found herself at odds with both their ideas and their behavior. In *We and Our Neighbors* Eva complains about the *"ambitious lady leaders"* who fail to see that "women's ordinary work" is just as important as men's work.[10] While Stowe felt that women should have opportunities beyond domestic labor, she consistently argued for the importance of women's domestic role. Sharply critical of certain inequities for women, she was also very traditional in some of her beliefs. And for this reason she seems ultimately to have felt alienated from the movement.

This alienation from the "lady leaders" is particularly apparent in the novel she published a few years later, *My Wife and I*. Several modern critics have taken for granted that the book satirizes Elizabeth Cady Stanton and Victoria Woodhull in the characters of Mrs. Cerulian and Miss Audacia Dagyereyes.[11] But in the preface to the first full-length edition of the novel, Stowe denied that any characters had been "designed as portraits of really existing individuals."[12] Miss Dagyereyes drinks and smokes and even visits Hal Henderson in his rooms, all of which seems to violate Stowe's notion of ladylike behavior. And Mrs. Cerulian is derided for supposing that "the ills of the world" would be solved by "giving the affairs of the world into the hands of women forthwith."[13] Stowe apparently feared that if women adopted the manners and values of men, they would be no better in positions of power. Instead she continued to argue that women's role was not to emulate men but rather to improve society by upholding their own beliefs and thereby influencing men to behave in a more humane way.

UNCLE TOM'S CABIN

Uncle Tom's Cabin has always been recognized for its exposé of slavery, but until quite recently few readers have paid much attention to either its literary merits or its feminist implications. While the slavery issue is central, it is not the only issue, and certainly it is not the main reason for reading *Uncle Tom's Cabin* today. *Uncle Tom's Cabin* makes clear the vital link between abolition and the women's rights movement, and in so doing has a historic importance that goes beyond the slavery issue. It is also America's first important epic novel, and whatever its shortcomings, it produced characters of such vividness that they have become an indelible part of America's literary tradition.

In a letter she wrote in 1853, Stowe stated explicitly that *Uncle Tom's Cabin* was intended as a *woman's* protest against slavery. "I wrote what I did," she said, "because as a woman, as a mother, I was oppressed and broken—with the sorrows of injustice I saw. . . . I must speak for the oppressed—who cannot speak for themselves."[14]

In narrating many episodes in the struggle against slavery during the period following the passage of the Fugitive Slave Law, the novel focuses principally on the separate adventures of two slaves, Uncle Tom and Eliza, both of whom are initially the property of Mr. Shelby, a cultured Southern gentleman. When Mr. Shelby's business affairs collapse, he is obliged to raise money by selling Tom and Eliza's little boy, Harry, to a ruthless slave trader. Unable to face the loss of her only child, Eliza runs off with him. Uncle Tom is so loyal to his master, however, that he willingly faces his destiny. As Stowe describes the lives of the two slaves after their departure from the Shelbys, it becomes increasingly clear that for Stowe abolition was a woman's cause. In the novel she calls slavery a "patriarchal institution,"[15] and *Uncle Tom's Cabin* demonstrates again and again that slavery is wrong principally because it destroys home and family, separating mothers and children, wives and husbands.

For Stowe, the primary guardians of the rights of black men and women were white women, who she believed had the sacred responsibility of instructing men to lead more virtuous lives. In the final pages of *Uncle Tom's Cabin* she wrote: "If the mothers of the free states had all felt as they should in times past, the sons of the free states would not have been the holders, and proverbially the hardest masters of slaves. . . . "[16] Thus it is women and mothers in particular who must lead the men who have the power. The idea was given fuller expression a few years later when Stowe declared:

The woman question of our day as I understand it is this—Shall MOTHERHOOD ever be felt in the public administration of the affairs of state? . . . The state at this very day needs an influence like what I remember our mothers' to have been . . . —an influence quiet, calm, warming, purifying, uniting. . . . it needs a loving and redeeming power, by which its erring and criminal children may be borne with, purified, and led back to virtue.[17]

How women's power can be used to combat the evil of slavery is shown again and again in *Uncle Tom's Cabin*. All of the women in the novel are mothers or surrogate mothers, and all but one, Marie St. Claire, argue in one way or another against slavery. Respectable white women try to use moral suasion to instruct men, who are the perpetrators of slavery, but when there is no other way, even law-breaking is shown as morally necessary.

In the early pages of the novel, two white women, both model wives and mothers, figure prominently: Mrs. Shelby and Mrs. Bird. They argue with obtuse husbands on behalf of the slaves, but they stop short of outright rebellion against their husbands' wishes. Mrs. Shelby, who is described as a woman who is in every way superior to her husband, is outraged on learning that in order to pay his debts Mr. Shelby plans to sell Tom and Eliza's little boy, Harry. She argues that the essential values are those of the family, not the market place, and she also condemns the laws and organized religion insofar as they support slavery. But Mr. Shelby is unimpressed by her arguments, and Mrs. Shelby, despite her moral outrage, acquiesces at least outwardly to male authority.

Since she cannot defy her husband, she resorts to undermining his efforts. In the character of Mrs. Shelby, Stowe demonstrates that the good wife, like the slave, does not wield authority; she can only plead, cajole, or even obstruct men's efforts, while men make the decisions. Thus when Haley, the slave trader, prepares to pursue Eliza after her escape with Harry, Mrs. Shelby and Aunt Chloe, the black cook, manage to use their wiles to delay him. Eliza succeeds in escaping, but Mrs. Shelby's efforts to persuade her husband to change his course of action fail. He accuses her of feeling too much, and an outraged Mrs. Shelby is left to explain to her unmoved listener what women and especially mothers must feel.

After fleeing from the Shelby household, Eliza seeks help along the way from Senator and Mrs. Bird, and once more there is a confrontation between husband and wife, in which the wife upholds the Bible and moral law while the husband attempts to argue for the Fugitive Slave Law, which he has been advocating in Congress. Mrs. Bird represents a motherly ideal, which will be repeated in other female characters later on. Her husband and children are her entire world, and because of the esteem in which her husband holds her, Mrs. Bird succeeds in persuading Senator Bird to help Eliza. Thus, like Mrs. Shelby, she does not rebel against male authority but accepts the notion that Stowe so often advances—that women must teach men to be morally better. While Mrs. Bird succeeds in this instance, hers is a limited victory since there is no indication that Senator Bird will hereafter work against, not for, the Fugitive Slave Law.

Yet another way in which women may fight "the patriarchal institution" of slavery is demonstrated by Miss Ophelia, who consents to go to the plantation of her brother, Augustine St. Claire, to help run a household that his incompetent wife has been neglecting. Miss Ophelia is supremely competent in all the domestic skills Stowe praised so highly in both the New York novels and *House and Home Papers*, but her efficiency is carried to ludicrous extremes until it is finally tempered by love. When we meet Miss Ophelia she is a caricature of a Calvinist minister, whose dedication to hard work makes her scarcely human. She was "as inevitable as a clock, and as inexorable as a railroad engine" (p. 245).

Miss Ophelia does not at first seem like very promising material, but she has a sense of morality which eventually permits her to overcome her racial prejudice. Furthermore, as an unmarried woman, she has the advantage of greater independence than the outraged wives in the novel. Like them, she argues the case against slavery on moral grounds, but she is ultimately more effective because she is able to take her stand without bowing to a husband's authority.

When Augustine puts his new purchase, Topsy, under the care of Miss Ophelia, she prevails upon him to assign Topsy's ownership to her so that she will have the authority to free her when she feels it appropriate. Augustine agrees, and Miss Ophelia in effect becomes a surrogate mother. She learns from her niece, Eva, that Topsy especially needs love, and Miss Ophelia assumes responsibilty. The result is that the unruly Topsy learns to be responsible and ultimately grows up to be a missionary. In effect, the power of motherhood overcomes the evils of slavery. But no properly married woman is able to exercise the same freedom of action that allows Miss Ophelia to translate her opposition to slavery into independent action.

Since for Stowe it is a woman's duty to oppose slavery, a woman who supports or condones it is not only villainous but a traitor to her sex. Marie St. Claire is such a woman. She does little but think about her "sick headaches" and go to church once a week in her most elegant finery. She fails her husband by caring little for his moral improvement; she fails her child by offering no love; and she fails as a woman because she accepts slavery and the rest of patriarchal society, which governs by expediency. We need only listen to Marie's complaints about her devoted slave Mammy to perceive her villainy. Marie asserts that she was "foolish and indulgent" when she did not insist that Mammy forget her husband and "marry" a new man. She blames Mammy for "obstinacy" when she refuses to marry in accord with her mistress's wishes and complains that Mammy would go back to her husband if permitted. As for Mammy's children, Marie explains that they had to be left with their father because "They were little dirty things" (p. 262). And as final evidence of her beneficence Marie tells Miss Ophelia that Mammy was not abused because she was whipped only once or twice in her life.

Although the evil slave trader Simon Legree has generally been regarded as the villain of the novel, Marie in her hypocrisy is at least as dangerous. In the end Marie is as responsible as Legree for Uncle Tom's death. Augustine had meant to free Tom, but when Augustine was killed, Marie refused to heed Miss Ophelia's entreaties on Tom's behalf and instead sold him to Legree. Had she behaved in accord with motherly values, she would have honored her husband's wishes and saved Tom. Instead, like the slave dealers, she values money over human happiness and unhesitatingly sacrifices him.

In this discussion of the women in *Uncle Tom's Cabin*, mention must be made of the Quaker, Rachel Halliday. Though her role is small, she is important because she most perfectly represents Stowe's womanly ideal. Free of the constraints of the Protestant church, she lives according to the teachings of the Bible and exemplifies the combined virtues of motherhood and Christianity. Rachael Halliday is described as a beautiful woman of fifty-five or sixty, who shines with inner goodness despite the drab shawl and dress she wears. The opposite of Marie St. Claire in appearance, she is also the opposite in behavior. She is the embodiment of "motherly loving kindness" (p. 215). Her home is domestic perfection, with its "singing teakettle" and its supper table covered with a "snowy cloth," laden with "plates of cake and saucers of preserves" (p. 221). Rachel and her husband are crucial to the plot in that they provide a way station on the underground railroad and, therefore, are instrumental in helping Eliza and her husband, George, escape, but they also serve in the novel as the archetype of human goodness, which is found in domestic perfection.

Though a small, perfect portrait, Rachel Halliday is still only a facilitator, not a major character. Kenneth Lynn has suggested that the real heroines of the novel are the black women.[18] They break the rules and in the end they prevail. In a world where women often could not hold property, had very limited access to the professions, were denied the right to vote, and were subject to the whims of their husbands, women and slaves had much in common. But the chief victim was the woman slave, who had to endure the indignities showered on both groups. The stories of Cassy and her daughter, Eliza, are poignant examples.

Cassy, a beautiful quadroon, passes from man to man, each in turn buying her for her sexual attractiveness. Two of her children are taken from her and sold, and she kills a third infant to protect herself and the child from further misery. Cassy denies piety, purity, submissiveness, and domesticity—all the ideals of True Womanhood expected in a patriarchal society. She is so proud and defiant that she even refutes the existence of God. And perhaps even more outrageous in the moral context of the novel, she is sexually free. She has been the mistress of several men against her will, but she admits that she willingly became the mistress of her first master because she loved him.

When we meet her in the novel, she is the slave of Simon Legree, but she is refusing his advances, preferring instead to work in the fields. She steals his money and in the end uses the only weapon she has, psychological torture, to defeat him. She persuades the superstitious Legree that his garret is haunted because years before he had confined a black woman there. Sandra M. Gilbert and Susan Gubar in *The Madwoman in the Attic* suggest that Cassy's elaborate scheme to frighten Legree in order that he may escape with his new concubine, Emmeline, is "the enactment of a uniquely female plot," that of the madwoman in the attic, the archetype of which is Bertha Mason, Rochester's mad wife in *Jane Eyre*.[19] Like Bertha, Cassy is a woman of passion who gains power over a man and ultimately secures retribution. But there the similarity stops. Although Cassy is described as partially insane, her actions, unlike Bertha's, indicate anything but insanity. Her carefully engineered plan works, and not only do she and Emmeline escape, but in addition she takes vengeance on the wicked Legree, who is seen in the end trembling with fright and calling on his dead mother, whose teachings he has so blatantly violated. Thus in transgressing all the limits of patriarchal society, Cassy alone not only escapes slavery but fights it and wins.

Eliza, when she chooses to flee with her little son, Harry, is like Cassy in her willingness to defy white society. In carrying Harry to freedom by crossing a treacherous river on floating pieces of ice, she exhibits a freedom and daring only equaled in the novel by Cassy. Nonetheless, Eliza adopts the conventional values of the white society in which she has been reared. She wants only to live in peace and harmony with her son and her husband, George, and she sees her role as helping George become a virtuous man. In his anger he has rejected God, but Eliza is a good Christian and manages to persuade George to return to the fold. Perceiving her moral virtue, George compliments her by calling her a "good child" (p. 85), a term which seems inappropriate for the heroine who risked her life crossing an icy river. Reunited with George, she is, however, satisfied to devote herself to his moral betterment and presumably to give up much of her own independence. The compromise for Stowe was acceptable because George is a good man and under Eliza's guidance presumably will become an even better one. While Stowe repeatedly shows the victimization of women who are dependent on bad or even morally inferior men, she stops short of arguing for the independence of all married women.

Central in Stowe's gallery of women is Eva, who though only a child embodies what Stowe shows throughout *Uncle Tom's Cabin* was the most important motherly value—love. "The gentle Eva," Stowe wrote, is "an impersonation in childish form of the love of Christ."[20] For Stowe, the Protestant church was one more manifestation of an oppressive patriarchy. Therefore, it is understandable that she chose to embody Christ in female form. The comparison of Eva to Christ is developed in a variety of ways. Tom "almost worshipped her as something heavenly and divine. He gazed on her as the Italian sailor gazes on his image of the child Jesus" (p. 379). Eva, like Christ, is willing to die to save mankind. Speaking of the slaves, she tells Tom, "I would die for them, Tom, if I could" (p. 400). Miss Ophelia calls Eva "Christ-like" (p. 411), and like Christ's disciples, Miss Ophelia learns from her. She tells Topsy, "I hope I've learned something of the love of Christ from her" (p. 432).

In her godliness Eva transcends the society in which she lives. Although she is born into a world where women are expected to influence but not to defy men, and where slaves have no rights at all, Eva manages to treat everyone equally. But equality is achieved only by the godly Eva. Expectations of both women and blacks fall short of that goal as each character in turn compromises with life's realities.

Inasmuch as the novel focuses so much on women, one might reasonably ask why Stowe made the title character a man. Elizabeth Ammons suggests that Tom is "a stereotypical Victorian heroine: pious, domestic, self-sacrificing, emotionally uninhibited in response to people and ethical questions." Thus, according to Ammons, he becomes "the supreme heroine of the book."[21] Like Eva, Tom is as close to God as a mortal can be. When Legree commands the beating that kills Tom, Christ-like, he cries out, "I forgive ye with all my soul!" (p. 584). If such godliness is a form of feminization, then to the extent that Tom is feminized he is a better man.

The world of *Uncle Tom's Cabin* is a mythic society where Uncle

Tom and various women characters attempt to introduce good amidst evil. The novel suggests that if there is hope for the future in this society, not only must women persuade men to be more loving, but they must help each other. Crises are resolved when women assist other women. Eliza is able to escape Haley, the slave trader, because Mrs. Shelby and Aunt Chloe succeed in detaining him. Along the way, she is helped by Senator Bird only because of Mrs. Bird's interference, and finally she finds sanctuary with the motherly Rachel Halliday. Cassy not only saves herself from Legree but also saves Emmeline. Miss Ophelia is responsible for the salvation of Topsy. And Eva is instrumental in Miss Ophelia's coming to understand that Topsy can be saved only through love.

The paradox in *Uncle Tom's Cabin* is that the women who try to change society by influencing men and thus play a woman's role, as defined by Stowe, are less effective than their more militant sisters. Miss Ophelia, Cassy, and Eliza, acting independently, manage to secure freedom from slavery. In contrast, Mrs. Shelby and Mrs. Bird, despite their considerable competence, are less successful because they rely on moral suasion alone. The book thus demonstrates that the gentle persuasion of women has limited influence, and that in a crisis it may be necessary to break the law, as do Cassy and Eliza, or to challenge male authority directly in the manner of Miss Ophelia.

Harriet Beecher Stowe herself was allegedly greeted by Lincoln as the "little woman who made the big war."[22] If indeed this often quoted statement is true, then it would be fair to say that few women in history who did not hold political power ever had greater influence on the men who governed. Thus Stowe may have succeeded in a way that her fictional women did not. *Uncle Tom's Cabin* did, in fact, present a mother's plea so that it reverberated in the United States and Europe. With the outstanding success of the novel, Stowe could have answered with a resounding "yes" to the Woman Question she had posed: "Shall MOTHERHOOD ever be felt in the public administration of the affairs of state?"

CRITICISM

The literature on *Uncle Tom's Cabin* is so enormous that it is impossible to review it all. What follows is an attempt to present the responses of some of the best-known critics and also to suggest the variety of viewpoints.

On the publication of *Uncle Tom's Cabin*, Stowe received letters of congratulation from such well-known literati as Whittier and Longfellow. Whittier thanked Stowe profusely for her "immortal book." And Longfellow exulted, "It is one of our greatest triumphs recorded in literary history, to say nothing of the higher triumph of its moral effect."[23]

Praise also came immediately from Europe. *The London Times* (1852) found *Uncle Tom's Cabin* "striking and meritorious," although the reviewer feared that it would stir up too much rancor and thereby defeat its own ends.[24] While the *Times* had reservations, two renowned women writers, George Sand and George Eliot, immediately welcomed Harriet Beecher Stowe to the company of leading writers of the time. George Sand (1852) wrote what she called not merely a review but an "homage," which was both "tender and spontaneous." Sand was the first of many critics to note that *Uncle Tom's Cabin* was primarily concerned with domesticity and the family and that it was particularly astute in its portrayal of women and children.[25] And a few years later George Eliot (1856) wrote a review of *Dred* in which she declared that *Uncle Tom* and *Dred* would assure Stowe "a place in the highest rank of novelists who can give us a national life in all its phases—popular and aristocratic, humorous and tragic, political and religious."[26]

The Northern and European monthlies were generally very favorable. The reviewer in *Putnam's Monthly* (1853) hailed *Uncle Tom's Cabin* as an important contribution to American literature, stating, "The great success of the book shows what may be accomplished by American authors who exercise their genius upon American subjects."[27] The *North American Review* was even more unstinting in its praise, calling the book "unquestioningly a work of genius," although the reviewer went on to complain that it was not of the caliber of Scott or Dickens.[28] *Blackwood's Edinburgh Magazine* (1853) was less equivocal, lauding Stowe's "undoubted genius." This reviewer not only found the book in some respects superior to any American predecessor or contemporary but argued: "There are, indeed, scenes and touches in this book which no living writer that we know of can surpass, and perhaps none ever equal."[29]

Southern monthlies were predictably less enthusiastic. One

Southern reviewer found the book threatening not only because of its position on slavery but because of its depiction of women. George F. Holmes, writing in the *Southern Literary Messenger* (1852), complained that Stowe was placing woman on a footing of political equality with man and thereby causing her "to look beyond the holy office of maternity," the result of which would be to hand the state over to "diplomatists and wet-nurse politicians."[30]

But despite detractors like Holmes, *Uncle Tom's Cabin* continued to gain the admiration of critics. John S. Hart in *Female Prose Writers of America* (1857) was lavish in his praise of Stowe's storytelling ability. "No living writer," he wrote, "equals her in abilities as a mere story teller, seizing the reader's attention, as she does, on the very first page, and holding it captive without any let-up to the very last."[31]

A later generation, including such notables as William Dean Howells, Charles Dudley Warner, Lev Tolstoi, Elizabeth Stuart Phelps, and Henry James, read *Uncle Tom's Cabin* with appreciation and even awe. William Dean Howells was especially impressed with Stowe's work. In 1895 he called *Uncle Tom's Cabin* "a very great novel . . . still perhaps our chief fiction," and he went on to praise the sentiment that later critics would dismiss as sentimentality.[32] Six years later he upheld his original judgment of the greatness of the novel, maintaining that it remained "almost the greatest work of the imagination we have produced in prose."[33]

Like Howells, Charles Dudley Warner (1896) found *Uncle Tom's Cabin* a work of tremendous significance because of its "insight into human nature" and "the fidelity to the facts of its own time." He therefore ranked it among the "works of genius."[34]

Elizabeth Stuart Phelps (1901) joined other women critics who saw in Stowe's work something distinctly female. She complained of "an insufficient estimate of Mrs. Stowe's value" which "sprung from the fact that she was a woman."[35]

Meanwhile, Tolstoi (1904–1912) included *Uncle Tom's Cabin* in a group of "models of a higher art which arises from the love of God and of our neighbor in the sphere of literature."[36] And Henry James (1913) seemed to sense a similar spirituality in the book when he called it "a state of vision of feeling and of consciousness" in which the reader participated fully and wholeheartedly.[37]

After more than a half century of criticism which by and large

indicated that *Uncle Tom's Cabin* was not only a good book but a
very great book, critical interest in the novel waned for an extended
period. Critics generally ignored the very qualities that had caused
generations to judge *Uncle Tom's Cabin* a work of genius. Stowe's
ability to draw character or to depict human emotions was barely
noticed. If *Uncle Tom's Cabin* was read at all, it was read for its
depiction of slavery. What had been perceived as the re-creation of
sincere emotional experience was now seen as "sentimentalism."
Vernon Parrington (1930) wrote somewhat condescendingly, "Despite its obvious blemishes of structure and sentimentalism, it is a
great document that stripped away the protective atmosphere from
the sacred institution and laid bare its elementary injustice."[38]

Uncle Tom's Cabin quickly slipped into oblivion until growing
concern with black identity in America sparked a reexamination.
James Baldwin (1949) insisted that the book badly misrepresented
the black character and thus contributed to racial prejudice. In addition, he complained that *Uncle Tom's Cabin* was "a very bad novel
having in its self-righteous virtuous sentimentality much in common with *Little Women*."[39] Baldwin's dim view of the book was by
no means echoed by all blacks. Indeed, Langston Hughes (1952)
commended Stowe's ability in developing strong narrative and sharp
characterization.[40] But the argument that Stowe distorted the black
character was taken up again by J. C. Furnas in a book entitled
Goodbye to Uncle Tom (1956).[41] The view that Uncle Tom suggests
the passivity and weakness of blacks still persists, but we have only
to turn back to Stowe's descriptions of the strong and kindly slave
to see that her intent was to suggest that Tom was not only a
superior but a godly man.

More contempt was heaped on *Uncle Tom's Cabin* by Leslie Fiedler (1960) when he turned his sardonic wit on "Little Eva" (a name
used in the unauthorized play based on the novel, but not by Stowe)
in an attempt to prove that Eva's deathbed scene was "prurient"
and even "pornographic."[42] Stowe surely would have been puzzled
by this view of what she clearly intended as an apotheosis.

Just when *Uncle Tom's Cabin* seemed to have reached a nadir among
critics, it began once more to be read with interest. Coming out of
a generation that had ignored Stowe, Edmund Wilson (1962) wrote
as if he had made a wonderful new discovery. He had some reservations about "the ineptitude of the prose," but admired the char-

acters and found the book "a much more impressive work than one
has ever been allowed to suspect."[43]

There followed an ongoing attempt to establish *Uncle Tom's Cabin*
as a work of aesthetic merit. Anthony Burgess (1966) called Stowe
the mother of both the protest novel and the literature of the South,
and went on to declare unequivocally that *Uncle Tom's Cabin* was
"a work of art."[44] Kenneth Lynn likewise praised the novel as art,
citing particularly "the truly Balzacian variousness of Mrs. Stowe's
characterizations."[45]

In the last decade a number of women critics have noted the
feminism in *Uncle Tom's Cabin*. Ellen Moers published several articles on Stowe and finally, in 1978, a book in which she firmly
declared that *Uncle Tom's Cabin* deserves a lasting place in American
literature because it is a "great novel." Like female critics of earlier
generations, Moers perceived what most criticism had ignored,
namely that Stowe believed that women could be instrumental in
achieving abolition by the way in which they lived their domestic
lives.[46] Ann Douglas (1981), while less enthusiastic about the novel,
nonetheless picked up on some of Moers's observations when she
called *Uncle Tom's Cabin* "a powerfully feminist book."[47]

The most complete analysis of Stowe's feminism is found at this
writing in Elizabeth Ammons's "Heroines in Uncle Tom's Cabin"
(1977). The genesis of Ammons's essay is a statement by Stowe made
on the death of her own child: "It was at his dying bed and at his
grave that I learned what a poor slave mother may feel when her
child is torn away from her."[48] Ammons goes on to point out that
maternal experience is at the center of the novel and that, as has
already been noted, Uncle Tom becomes a heroine rather than a
hero in the tradition of the "Adamic rebel" in the American novel.[49]

What emerges from the combined feminist criticism is a view
that Stowe herself stated clearly and that has been elaborated here
but which has nonetheless been largely ignored by critics until now,
namely that Stowe wrote out of her experience as a mother, and
she addressed *Uncle Tom's Cabin* particularly to mothers, who she
felt ought to exercise leadership in the struggle against slavery. Her
argument is developed in the novel mainly in her female characterizations.

While Stowe was not always in sympathy with the women's rights
movement of her time, her writings indicate that she shared with

movement leaders a desire for greater opportunities for women so that they might lead more useful lives. But she went even beyond most of them in assuming that women could exercise political power by instilling virtue into men and thereby become instrumental in creating a better world. These ideas are scattered throughout many of Stowe's writings, but the evidence presented here suggests that her most well defined statement on the Woman Question is in *Uncle Tom's Cabin*.

Furthermore, it should be clear that *Uncle Tom's Cabin* can no longer be shunted aside as an anti-slavery novel and, therefore, a mere period piece. The diverse critical opinion indicates at the very least that it holds a unique place in American literature.

NOTES

1. Barbara M. Cross, "Stowe, Harriet Beecher," *Notable American Women 1607–1950* (Cambridge, Mass.: Belknap Press, 1971).

2. John R. Adams, *Harriet Beecher Stowe* (New York: Twayne, 1963), p. 27.

3. "To George Eliot," May 25, 1896, as quoted in Edward Wagenknecht, *Harriet Beecher Stowe: The Known and the Unknown* (New York: Oxford University Press, 1965), p. 97.

4. Jean Ashton claims, "Her actions and statements often point in different directions" (*Harriet Beecher Stowe: A Reference Guide* [Boston: G. K. Hall, 1977], p. xi). Dorothy Berkson says, "She was at the very least ambivalent about what she (like others) called "The Woman Question" ("Millennial Politics and the Feminine Fiction of Harriet Beecher Stowe," in *Critical Essays on Harriet Beecher Stowe*, ed. Elizabeth Ammons [Boston: G. K. Hall, 1980], p. 251).

5. Harriet Beecher Stowe, "What Will You Do with Her? or The Woman Question," in *Household Papers and Stories* (Boston: Houghton Mifflin, 1896), pp. 232–35.

6. Harriet Beecher Stowe, "Woman's Sphere," in *Household Papers*, p. 254.

7. Harriet Beecher Stowe, *Hearth and Home* (1868) as quoted in Wagenknecht, *Harriet Beecher Stowe*, p. 97.

8. Harriet Beecher Stowe, *My Wife and I* (New York: J. B. Ford, 1871), p. 239.

9. Harriet Beecher Stowe, *Lady Byron Vindicated* (Boston: Fields, Osgood, 1870), p. 120.

10. Harriet Beecher Stowe, *We and Our Neighbors* (1875; rpt. Boston: Houghton Mifflin, 1900), p. 36.

11. See, for example, John R. Adams, *Harriet Beecher Stowe* (New York: Twayne, 1963), p. 85; and Alice C. Crozier, *The Novels of Harriet Beecher Stowe* (New York: Oxford University Press, 1969), p. 185.

12. Stowe, *My Wife and I*, p. 231.

13. Ibid.

14. "To Lord Chief Denman," January 20, 1853, Huntington Library, as quoted in Ellen Moers, *Harriet Beecher Stowe and American Literature* (Hartford: Stowe-Day, 1978), p. 22.

15. Stowe uses the term "patriarchal" without suggesting the perjorative meaning that it has been given by modern feminist theorists. Nevertheless, the term is significant for its literal meaning because it is mainly the fathers in the novel who advocate slavery, while the mothers generally oppose it.

16. Harriet Beecher Stowe, *Uncle Tom's Cabin; or, Life Among the Lowly*, Intro. by Ann Douglas, ed. (New York: Penguin, 1981), p. 624. All further references to this work will be indicated parenthetically within the text.

17. Stowe, *My Wife and I*, pp. 37–38.

18. Kenneth Lynn, *Visions of America* (Westport, Conn.: Greenwood Press, 1973), p. 48.

19. Sandra M. Gilbert and Susan Gubar, *The Madwoman in the Attic: The Woman Writer and the Nineteenth-Century Literary Imagination* (New Haven: Yale University Press, 1979), p. 534.

20. Harriet Beecher Stowe, *The Key to Uncle Tom's Cabin* (Boston: John B. Jewett, 1854), p. 51.

21. Elizabeth Ammons, "Heroines in Uncle Tom's Cabin," *American Literature* 49 (May 1977): 16–79, rpt. in *Critical Essays on Harriet Beecher Stowe*, p. 159.

22. These words—with slight variation—are frequently quoted without a source.

23. As quoted in Forrest Wilson, *Crusader in Crinoline: The Life of Harriet Beecher Stowe* (New York: J. B. Lippincott, 1941), p. 283.

24. Review of *Uncle Tom's Cabin*, *Times* (London) September 3, 1852, p. 5, rpt. in *Critical Essays on Harriet Beecher Stowe*, p. 26.

25. George Sand, review of *Uncle Tom's Cabin*, *La Presse*, December 17, 1852, rpt. in *Critical Essays on Harriet Beecher Stowe*, p. 2.

26. George Eliot, review of *Dred; a Tale of the Great Dismal Swamp*, *Westminster Review* 10 (October 1856), 571-73, rpt. in *Critical Essays on Harriet Beecher Stowe*, p. 44.

27. "Uncle Tomitudes," *Putnam's Monthly* 1 (January 1853); 97–102, rpt. in *Critical Essays of Harriet Beecher Stowe*, p. 40.

28. Review of *Uncle Tom's Cabin*, *North American Review* 77 (October 1853): 466.

29. Review of *Uncle Tom's Cabin*, *Blackwood's Edinburgh Magazine* 74 (October 1853): 395.

30. George F. Holmes, review of *Uncle Tom's Cabin*, *Southern Literary Messenger* 18 (October 1852): 630–38, rpt. in *Critical Essays on Harriet Beecher Stowe*, p. 8.

31. John S. Hart, *Female Prose Writers of America* (Philadelphia: E. H. Butler, 1857), p. 287.

32. William Dean Howells, *My Literary Passions*, Library Edition of the *Writings of William Dean Howells* (New York: Harper, 1895), p. 50.

33. William Dean Howells, "Literary Boston as I Knew It," in *Literary Friends and Acquaintances* (New York: Harper, 1901), pp. 115–18, 138–40, rpt. in *Critical Essays on Harriet Beecher Stowe*, p. 280.

34. Charles Dudley Warner, review of *Uncle Tom's Cabin*, *Atlantic Monthly* 78 (July 1896): 311–21, rpt. in *Critical Essays on Harriet Beecher Stowe*, p. 72.

35. Elizabeth Stuart Phelps, *Chapters from a Life* (New York: Houghton Mifflin, 1901), pp. 131–38 , rpt. in "Mrs. Stowe," in *Critical Essays on Harriet Beecher Stowe*, p. 283.

36. Lev N. Tolstoi, *What Is Art?* Vol. 22 of *Works by Count Lev N. Tolstoi*, trans. Leo Wiener (Boston: Colonial Press, 1904–1912), pp. 299–300, rpt. in Ellen Moers, Epigraph, *Harriet Beecher Stowe and American Literature* (Hartford: Stowe-Day, 1978).

37. Henry James, *A Small Boy and Others* (New York: Charles Scribner's, 1913), pp. 158–60.

38. Vernon Parrington, "Harriet Beecher Stowe, a Daughter of Puritanism," *Main Currents in American Thought*, Vol. 2 (New York: Harcourt, Brace, 1930), pp. 372–78, rpt. in *Critical Essays on Harriet Beecher Stowe*, p. 217.

39. James Baldwin, "Everybody's Protest Novel," *Partisan Review* 16 (June 1949): 578–85, rpt. in *Critical Essays on Harriet Beecher Stowe*, p. 92.

40. Langston Hughes, Introduction, *Uncle Tom's Cabin* (New York: Dodd, Mead, 1952), pp. i–iii, rpt. in *Critical Essays on Harriet Beecher Stowe*, p. 103.

41. J. C. Furnas, *Goodbye to Uncle Tom* (New York: William Morrow, 1956).

42. Leslie Fiedler, *Love and Death in the American Novel* (New York: Stein & Day, 1960), pp. 264–69.

43. Edmund Wilson, *Patriotic Gore: Studies in the Literature of the American Civil War* (New York: Oxford University Press, 1962), pp. 3–11.

44. Anthony Burgess, "Making de White Boss Frown," *Encounter* 27

(July 1966): 54–58, rpt. in *Critical Essays on Harriet Beecher Stowe*, pp. 122–23.

45. Lynn, *Visions of America*, p. 32.

46. Ellen Moers, *Harriet Beecher Stowe and American Literature* (Hartford, Conn.: Stowe-Day, 1978).

47. Ann Douglas, Introduction, *Uncle Tom's Cabin: or, Life Among the Lowly*, p. 13.

48. Charles Edward Stowe, *Life of Harriet Beecher Stowe, Compiled from Her Letters and Journals* (Boston and New York: Gale Research Co., 1889), p. 104.

49. Ammons, "Heroines in Uncle Tom's Cabin," p. 152.

3

Work and the Bridging of Social Class: Elizabeth Stuart Phelps, *The Silent Partner* (1871)

In 1871, the year she published *The Silent Partner*, Elizabeth Stuart Phelps called the Woman Question "the most important question God had ever asked the world since he asked 'What think ye of Christ on Calvary!' "[1] A few weeks later she wrote in a letter: "I am, as perhaps you may suppose almost *invested* in the 'Woman Cause.' It grows upon my conscience, as well as my enthusiasm every day. It seems to me to be the first work God has to be done just now."[2] An understanding of Phelps's commitment to the Woman Question is central to the study of her life and work.

Born in 1844 in Boston, Massachusetts, Phelps was raised in Andover, Massachusetts, where her father, Austin Phelps, and her maternal grandfather, Moses Stuart, were professors of sacred literature at Andover Theological Seminary. She was baptized Mary Gray Phelps, but after the death of her beloved mother she took her name, Elizabeth Stuart. Growing up in an enormous house, which still stands on Andover Hill, Phelps enjoyed the life of a Boston Brahmin, modified somewhat by the stern Calvinist doctrine that was upheld in the family. While her work and public statements suggest that Phelps adhered to many aspects of that doctrine, at least one critic, Christine Stansell, has suggested that her first novel, *The Gates Ajar* (1868), was intended as a rejection of her father's religion.[3]

The more important parental influence on Phelps seems to have been her mother, who despite ill health struggled to be both writer and loving parent. When Phelps was only eight her beloved mother died shortly after publishing her fourth book and giving birth to her third child. In writing about her mother in her autobiographical *Chapters from a Life*, Phelps spoke admiringly of her efforts to reconcile her career and her domestic life, but she attributed her mother's death to the struggle between her art and her household duties.[4] Later Phelps explored this conflict in detail in her novel *The Story of Avis*, which was clearly based on the life of the elder Elizabeth Stuart Phelps. Avis was Phelps's favorite heroine, and the story in which she figured was for Phelps "a woman's book," which she did not expect men to value or even to comprehend.[5]

Phelps attributed her decision to become a writer not only to her mother's example but to her reading of Elizabeth Barrett Browning's verse-novel *Aurora Leigh*, a work in which the heroine rejects her adoring suitor because she wishes to be a poet and to define her own life. Like Aurora Leigh, Phelps would assert her independence through her writing.

Phelps was only thirteen when she began publishing juvenile fiction, and she continued to publish juvenile fiction for the next several years until 1864, when her first adult story appeared in *Harper's*. In that year she also began her first and most popular novel, *The Gates Ajar*. Although the book received mixed reviews, it sold more copies than any other nineteenth-century novel except *Uncle Tom's Cabin*. Thereafter she wrote prolifically, publishing a total of fifty-seven books besides fiction, poetry, and articles for magazines.

Most of the articles she published in periodicals, and in particular a weekly series she contributed to the *Independent* from July 13 to October 12, 1871, dealt with women's issues, including suffrage, clothes, health, education, work, and marriage. Of all the problems she addressed, the question of work for women seems to have been paramount. She lamented "[w]oman's monetary helplessness," and complained about women's inability to choose their own work and position.[6]

Addressing primarily female readers in an article in *Harper's* she urged them to seek congenial work of their own and took to task those fathers who forbid their daughters to seek paid employment. She warned such fathers that while they encouraged their sons, they were dwarfing their daughters' souls.

But despite her certainty that work was essential to women, she continued to express concern that it was difficult, if not impossible, for a woman to meet the conflicting demands of family and career. Undoubtedly haunted by her mother's experience, she remained concerned that it was not feasible for a woman with a family to be a successful writer.[7] Indeed, she seemed throughout her life to resent her mother's sacrifice. "[U]nder the movement of a nature like hers a woman may make a man divinely happy," she wrote in 1891. "But," she added wryly, "she may die in trying to do so."[8]

The issues of women's lives which Phelps explored in so many articles inevitably found further expression in her fiction. According to Mari Jo Buhle and Florence Howe, Phelps's fiction reflected the agenda of the Declaration of Sentiments ratified at Seneca Falls in that her major concerns were the rights of women to equal educational opportunity, satisfying work, and political equality.[9]

Carol Farley Kessler suggests that not only are women's concerns reflected in Phelps's fiction, but the questions raised from novel to novel have close parallels with Phelps's own life. She observes, for example, that before 1877 Phelps's female protagonists refuse marriage. Between 1877 and 1881 they accept marriage "but with unfortunate and ambiguous results." And from 1887 onward male protagonists expect emotional support from women in marriage.[10] This development reflects Phelps's own development. Initially she enjoyed the independence of her single life, but with the breakdown of her health in her forties she seemed to desire a lifelong companion. Thus in 1888, at the age of forty-four, Phelps married Herbert Dickinson Ward, a writer seventeen years her junior. Early in the marriage they collaborated on three Biblical romances, but over the years the marriage disintegrated.

Although the Woman Question loomed large for Phelps, she did not actively participate in the women's rights movement. Instead she sought to make her contribution through writing. She lamented that history was written by man and was, therefore, "capricious in its treatment of women." Like feminists today, she recalled the history of the Pilgrim fathers only to wonder about the Pilgrim mothers. And she complained that we know so little of our heroines.[11] In writing fiction, Phelps clearly intended to correct some of the wrongs of history. Her heroines are strong women who she hoped would serve as an inspiration to the many women readers of her time. She succeeded in this aspiration because when she died at age sixty-six, she was a widely read and well-respected writer.

THE SILENT PARTNER

In her preface to *The Silent Partner*, Phelps stated that her intent was to call attention to the abuses of our factory system, especially as exhibited in many of the country mills. She failed to note, however, that her critique was from a decidedly feminine perspective. Mari Jo Buhle and Florence Howe point out that "Phelps located the dynamic of the Woman Question within a specific historical context, namely the emergence of industrial capitalism" (p. 371). Large numbers of women labored in the mills, enduring terrible conditions for low pay, and it was these women above all who engaged Phelps's interest and concern.

The Silent Partner is the story of two women, Perley Kelso, the daughter of a wealthy mill owner, and Sip Garth, an impoverished mill hand. As the novel opens, Perley is seen "sitting before a fire" (p. 11), almost a symbol of docile, confined womanhood. Outside there has been a long storm, but Perley does not need "to dampen the soles of her delicate sandals" (p. 11) to go beyond her privileged position. The turbulence of the world at large does not impinge on the sheltered existence of Miss Kelso.

The authorial voice, distanced and satiric, suggests that Perley is to be viewed with disdain:

If, in addition to the circumstances of being twenty-three, you are the daughter of a gentleman manufacturer, and a resident of Boston, it would hardly appear that you require the ceremony of an introduction. A pansy-bed in the sun would be a difficult subject of classification. (Pp. 9–10)

A Boston Brahmin herself, Phelps nonetheless had contempt for the privilege of birth. A woman who was merely "a pansy-bed in the sun" was an object of contempt.

The description of Perley continues to emphasize her vacuity. Her hands are folded, and she is "sitting, as she had been sitting all the opaque, gray afternoon, in a crimson chair by a crimson fire, a creamy profile and a creamy hand lifted and cut between the

two foci of color. . . . The hand had—rings" (p. 10). She is a painting in lovely contrasting colors—a beautiful object—quietly posed,
hands folded as though inanimate, the whole devoid of life. The
useless hands serve merely to show off her rings. Her face is mentioned only as a profile, suggesting a lack of interior vitality.

Perley is bored. She is uncertain whether or not to go to the
opera on this rainy night, but finally decides to go. Having made
this decision, she has nothing left to occupy her mind. And there
seems to be equally little in Perley's heart. Soon after the scene
described above, Perley learns of the death of her father, about
which she comments to her fiancé, Maverick: "I'm not used you
know, Maverick, to feeling at all; it's never been asked of me before" (p. 39). It is as if Perley as a young woman is little more than
a baby, unable to think or feel beyond a very superficial level. But
as the novel progresses, Perley teaches herself to become a fully
adult human being. Thus, on one level the novel is the story of a
young woman's self education.

Education begins in earnest when Perley suggests that she should
look after her own property. Maverick, who is not only her fiancé
but also a partner in her late father's firm, greets her suggestion
with laughter. She is also met with derision by the senior partner,
Mr. Hayle, when she suggests that she ought to be named a partner. Her reaction is to feel "ashamed of being a woman" (p. 59).
To the men, women are mere children, who are not to be taken
seriously. Perley is told that all she can be is a silent partner. She
may benefit from the money earned by the mills, but she is denied
the opportunity to be an active worker. She is not consoled by Mr.
Hayle's condescending remark, "Business obligation and responsibility are always so trying to a lady" (p. 60).

Perley reasons that there is nothing in the law that forbids a
woman from becoming an active partner, and she is determined to
resist Maverick, who admits that she is disqualified on the sole ground
that she is "a young lady." Her only recourse is to somehow prove
not only that she is qualified but that she is, in fact, more qualified
than a man.

She accomplishes this objective by embarking on a life devoted
to improving the lot of the mill workers. In so doing she develops
in herself what Phelps considered the special "feminine strength."
For Phelps there was strength in tenderness, and Perley becomes

increasingly strong as she learns to minister to the needs of the workers.

The partners, however, remain blind to Perley's growing strength. They refuse to discuss major issues with her and consult her only on a question of whether the mouldings should be of Gloucester granite or not. Perley responds bitterly to one partner: "You see, Mr. Garrick, when you are a woman and a silent partner, it is only the mouldings of a matter that fall to you" (p. 143). It remains for Perley to demonstrate that she can do more than concern herself with the "mouldings of a matter."

The opportunity for Perley to prove herself develops when the workers decide to strike. The partners are powerless in the face of the strike decision, but Perley is able to prevail, and the strike is averted. Perley's earlier philanthropic efforts on behalf of the workers have earned their trust, so that they listen only to her when she appears with the other partners at a workers' meeting. In the scene where Perley, the silent partner, finally finds her voice, she stands "in the mud in the rain" (p. 250). Thus symbolically she enters into the real world of suffering and discomfort from which she had retreated in the novel's opening scene, where she was keeping her delicate sandals dry while the storm raged outside. The fully realized woman does not retreat.

The workers understand that Perley has entered their world, and they listen with awe and respect. To the astonishment of the male partners, the workers not only decide not to strike but agree to a wage reduction in order to keep the company solvent. Perley thus becomes an active partner who brings a woman's special skills to the task.

As Perley begins to assert herself, she becomes aware that she does not love Maverick. Recognizing that she has changed, she talks of "a growing away." Maverick is sad and disappointed but must accept her decision. The authorial voice comments:

He would probably have loved her without a question, and rested in her, without a jar, to his dying day. A man often so loves and rests in a superior woman. He thinks himself to be the beach against which she frets herself; he is the wreck which she has drowned. (P. 163)

In an era where marriage was viewed as a woman's sole destiny, these words seem strikingly revolutionary. But even the nineteenth-century reader probably would have agreed that Maverick Hayle no longer appeared to be a suitable husband for Perley.

The marriage issue becomes more complex when Perley receives a proposal from Mr. Garrick. Mr. Garrick is a man of kindness and intelligence for whom Perley develops great respect, but he too must be refused because Perley sees no way of reconciling marriage with her lifework. She tells him that since love and marriage are a business or trade for women, she must remain alone so that she can do the work she values.

In contrasting her life choice with that of other women, she delivers what amounts to a diatribe against marriage. Perley observes that other women are lonely, sick, homeless, and miserable, while she is happy and busy. She tells Garrick that if she married him, she "should invest in life," and he "would conduct it." Instead she says she has "a preference for a business of my own" (p. 261).

In eschewing marriage, Perley feels she is losing nothing that she values. By contrast, the lives of other wealthy women in the book look dull and pointless. Mrs. Silver and Miss Kenna, Perley's one-time friends, wring their hands over her. They complain that her home is not that of a young lady but something akin to a hospital or a set of public soup rooms. They describe her life as "morbid," but Perley does not care. She has sacrificed the petty advantages of society, and in return she has secured the love of the poor and disadvantaged.

The final portrait of Perley contrasts sharply with that in the opening scene of the novel. Perley's face is now "healthy" and "happy." It is a "womanly, wonderful face" that is "opulent and warm" and brimming with life (p. 302). Her interior rather than exterior beauty is revealed. She has found happiness by giving love and compassion where needed.

The portrait of Sip Garth is less fully etched than that of Perley, but in many ways it is a companion piece. Through Sip we are intended to see how a woman at the opposite end of the social scale from Perley can develop her strength and likewise find happiness.

The first view of Sip, like the first view of Perley, is very telling. On the rainy night on which Perley decided to go to the opera, she glanced from her carriage and was fascinated by "the manful struggles of a girl in a plaid dress, who battled with the gusts about a carriage length ahead of her." She seems to Perley to be "like a desperate prize-fighter" in her struggle to keep her balance (p. 17). Sip's life is indeed that of a desperate prizefighter who persists in the struggle and with great difficulty hangs on despite tremendous adversity.

She was born to an overworked mother and drunken father, who beat her and her sister. There were originally six children in the family, but the only survivors are Sip and Catty, a deaf-mute, who Sip must care for as if she were a child. As though that were not enough, by the middle of the novel it becomes apparent that Catty is losing her eyesight. A visit to the eye doctor reveals that her eyes have been contaminated by a toxic substance used in the factory, and she is destined to go blind.

Sip, like other factory workers at the Hayle and Kelso mills, goes to work from half past six in the morning to seven at night. She is a "hand," that is, "the fingers of the world," denied the valid existence of either "head or heart" (p. 71). She works in a cold or "morbidly hot" room, eats cold lunch, and wanders home to a smelly, damp tenement at night. Although Sip is a determined fighter, she cannot fight alone, and in the end she is able to endure because of the support given her by Perley.

Having learned from Sip of her hard life, Perley one evening arrives at Sip's quarters shortly before the latter returns from work. When Sip finally comes home, she finds Perley with her kid gloves off and a poker in her hands, making a fire for the first time in her life. The symbolic gesture marks the beginning of Perley's efforts to give up a world of leisure so that she can bring comfort to the sordid lives of the mill hands. In return Sip is able to show Perley how she can in her own way move from silent partner to active partner in the mills.

Sip has a worldly wisdom and frankness that enable her to point out to the as yet naive Perley that despite her deceased father's wealth and position, she herself has done little in the world. Perley is surprised initially that the mill hands do not treat her with interest or respect until Sip explains that she must advance her cause through her own independent efforts.

In turn, Perley provides the inspiration to Sip to find her life-work. Sip spies an engraving of Lemude's dreaming Beethoven in Perley's room, and she interprets the picture as a vision of Beethoven unable to master the orchestra which is riding over him and sweeping him along. Beethoven fights, but he cannot stop the relentless motion. Sip compares this to the ideas she would articulate if she had the chance. Perley eventually gives Sip the picture, which comes to symbolize Sip's own efforts to break the silence and give voice to the ideas that overwhelm her.

Sip is finally able to state these ideas when at the end she becomes a preacher. Her doctrine is simple. She denies what she calls "rich religion," bluntly cursing the rich folk and their beliefs. Like Stowe and other writers considered here, Phelps challenges the religion of her forefathers. Both her father and grandfather, as professors at Andover Theological Seminary, were foremost advocates of "rich religion," but Phelps conceives of religion as something quite different. The religion that Sip teaches is simply a doctrine of love, which she claims she learned from her deaf-mute sister, Catty.

In her dumb sullenness Catty symbolizes the hopeless mill hands who can neither fully understand nor express their misery. She represents a world that is "deaf, dumb, blind, doomed, stepping confidently to its own destruction before our eyes" (pp. 277–78).

Despite her overwhelming problems, Catty can be reached by love. When Sip patiently spells on Catty's fingers the words "for love's sake," the sullen, ill-tempered girl repeats the words and gently lays her head in Sip's lap. As love humanizes Catty, so later on will it humanize the mill hands to whom Sip preaches. It seems that women alone are able to convey the all-important love which is central to life.

What begins to emerge is a community of women supporting one another in a world that men either will not or cannot understand. When Sip learns that Catty will soon be blind, she seeks "women-folks" to cry to. It is Perley who responds to Sip's need by holding and kissing her. Having once been comforted, Sip is soon able to rise to the challenge. She resolves that she will help Catty by working. But Catty cannot be saved, even by Sip's love. When the town is deluged by a flood toward the end of the novel, Catty drowns.

With Catty gone, Sip is free to pursue her own future. The first possibility that is presented to her is a marriage proposal from a kind and ambitious fellow worker, Dirk. But Sip refuses him because she does not wish to bring children into the world to live the kind of life she has lived as a factory worker. Instead Sip resolves that she will remain single so that she can devote herself to reforming the world in which she lives. To propagate the man-made values she has lived with seems wrong to her. We are assured at the end that she will be "a very happy woman" (p. 291).

The Silent Partner in its tale of two women suggests that if there is hope of a better world, that hope will be realized as women find their voices and bring love to a patriarchal society in which human values are disregarded. If the plot verges on a kind of sentimentality that characterized the woman's novel a generation earlier, its implications are more profound. Mari Jo Buhle and Florence Howe suggest that *The Silent Partner* is "extraordinary" because it is a woman-centered novel focusing not on domestic life and romance but rather on industry and women's vocations. And it presents women in a new light as "strong caretakers" (pp. 381–82).

But *The Silent Partner* is more than a polemic. Phelps, like other women writers of her time, wrote in a realistic style in an effort to re-create the horror and angst of the world she observed. The scenes of the mill hands in particular have a pictorial quality that is as compelling as anything in American literature. Consider, for example, the description of the death of a poor child while he is working in the mills:

There is a spring and a cry. Bub has pounced upon Bill's torn pocket. Bill has backed, and dragged him. The wagging rag on Bub's little trousers has caught in a belt.

All over the spoiling-room there is a spring and a cry.

All up the stairs there seems to be a spring and a cry. They come from the song about the Happy, Happy Day. The engines close teeth on the song and the child together.

They stop the machinery; they run to and fro; they huddle together; they pick up something here, and wipe up something there, and cover up something yonder, closely; they look at one another with white faces; they sit down sickly; they ask what is to do next.

There is nothing to do. Bub has saved the state his two hundred and fifty dollars, and has Bill's quid of tobacco in his mangled hand. There is nothing to do. Life, like everything else, was quite too young for Bub. He has got so old, he has given it up. (Pp. 215–16)

In addition to the close attention to detail, there is here a pointed attempt to re-create the speed of events and the confusion through short sentences and repetition. There is also a careful attention to style that belies much of the criticism, which insists that Phelps, like other women writers, was merely a popular novelist whose work lacks aesthetic quality. Like Stowe, Phelps believed that the novel must inform more than entertain. Nonetheless, she had a grasp of language and situation which ought not to be dismissed.

CRITICISM

Barely known today, Elizabeth Stuart Phelps was well recognized during her lifetime. She herself shyly mentioned early praise received from Whittier, Thomas Wentworth Higginson, and Longfellow. She never tells us precisely what these noted gentlemen wrote, but she assures us that Whittier and Higginson "said the pleasant thing which goes so far towards keeping the courage of young writers above sinking point, and which to a self-distrustful nature, may be little less than a life-preserver." Of Longfellow she wrote only that he was "very kind." [12]

At least one brief comment by Higginson survives in his essay "Late Books by American Women" (1871), in which he wrote that Phelps was a writer of "more genius" than either Alcott or Stowe but complained that she "is led on by her own fiery earnestness and intense purpose to a similar disregard of literary execution." [13]

Other comments on the publication of *The Silent Partner* in 1871 were generally more favorable both here and abroad. In London the *Athenaeum* praised the characterization of Perley and found occasional eloquence in the novel. [14] And on this side of the Atlantic, *Literary World* commended the novel's realism and the characterizations of Perley and Sip. [15] While *Harper's* was somewhat less enthusiastic, the editors nonetheless found it "effective and artistic" and "the best . . . of Miss Phelps's novels." [16]

During her lifetime Phelps was also favorably acknowledged by literary critic Bliss Perry (1902), who identified Elizabeth Stuart Phelps, along with Mrs. Stowe, Miss Jewett, and Miss Wilkins, as "excellent" New England writers. [17] Such comments always, of course, have a double edge insofar as women writers are dumped into a category that seems to exclude them from the mainstream of American literature.

After Phelps's death in 1911, her reputation seems to have declined somewhat, but for a time she continued to be accorded recognition, notably by Fred Lewis Pattee. In 1915 he wrote, "It is impossible to read her with calmness: one is shocked and grieved and harrowed; one is urged on every page to think, to feel, to rush forth and fight some wrong, to condemn some evil or champion some cause."[18] For Pattee Phelps's concern with social issues did not preclude the possibility of aesthetic achievement. In 1923 he added, "No other woman of the period may be compared with Miss Phelps for sheer literary power—the power that feels a situation and makes a reader feel."[19] One wonders how Pattee would have ranked Phelps with men of the period, but the placing of women in separate categories was endemic, and Pattee's response is notable for its enthusiasm.

Soon after Pattee wrote so favorably of Phelps's fiction, interest in her work became minimal. Where she was mentioned at all, it was often with condescension or disparagement, although she was still occasionally acknowledged for her attempt to call attention to factory conditions. Vernon Parrington (1927–1930) wrote, "*The Silent Partner* is an emotional Puritan document that was out of date when it came from the press."[20] And John Macy (1931) included Phelps in a list of "names which are dropping farther from sight every year."[21] Arthur Hobson Quinn (1936) was more laudatory, but even he had reservations. He commented, "*The Silent Partner* has scenes that are unsurpassed in English fiction except in the pages of Charles Dickens," but he added, "the most serious criticism of Mrs. Ward lies in a certain monotony of subject and tone."[22] The comparison to Dickens is typical insofar as women novelists writing in the realistic genre were frequently complimented for their affinities with the acknowledged master. Indeed, one is tempted to add that Dickens, for all his realistic depictions of character and place, could be sentimental and didactic, the very qualities so often faulted in women novelists.

Criticism of the next decade continued to recognize Phelps, but without much enthusiasm. Van Wyck Brooks (1940) noted that Phelps's "short stories, *Fourteen to One*, were often poignant and skillful; but the tone of her work in general was too consciously righteous."[23] And in a reappraisal of Phelps in 1951, Arthur Hobson Quinn noted her similarity to Rebecca Harding Davis in her attempts to picture the "human cost of industrialism, especially in terms of the woman mill-workers."[24]

Thus while Phelps was not entirely forgotten, she was certainly relegated to a very minor place in American letters. In her recent book, *Elizabeth Stuart Phelps* (1982), Carol Farley Kessler explains that Phelps's reputation declined because her central cause was women, a subject which critics found "embarrassing." Moreover, according to Kessler, women's writing is generally ignored unless "clearly superior in its belletristic attributes."[25] One is tempted to add that women's writing, especially that of nineteenth-century American women, has been ignored regardless.

If Kessler is right, then Elizabeth Stuart Phelps suffered the same fate as other women writers facing a male critical establishment, which seemed to have difficulty in validating the female perspective and the woman-centered novel. Phelps herself recognized the problem in her own time when, as mentioned previously, she voiced suspicion that Stowe was probably undervalued because she was a woman. And both Longfellow and James T. Fields earned her praise for their ability to judge a woman's work on its merits.

With the rise of the women's rights movement in the 1960s there has been renewed interest in Elizabeth Stuart Phelps, particularly among women critics, who have been fascinated by the outspoken feminism that eluded several generations of male critics. Despite what she called "shabby plots and platitudinous melodrama," Christine Stansell (1972) commended Phelps for her "devastating analysis of the nature of heterosexuality and its implications for the liberation of women."[26]

The year 1973 saw the publication of a substantial excerpt from Phelps's *The Story of Avis* in an anthology by Lee Edwards and Arlyn Diamond, who regard Phelps as one of several women who form an American literary tradition in fiction quite different from that created by male writers. This fiction is identified as "psychological" rather than "cosmological" and characterized by a "sense of conflict" created by women's difficulties in reconciling their private selves with public expectations of them as women.[27]

Carol Farley Kessler (1982) pursues the argument that Phelps's special contribution is in her talent for revealing women's lives. For this reason Kessler suggests that Phelps deserves particular attention from cultural historians and literary sociologists.[28]

Mari Jo Buhle and Florence Howe (1983) also consider that Phelps is noteworthy because, in writing of the female experience in America, she was contributing to a long-neglected but significant aspect of American literature, the separate and distinct world of women as she herself knew them (pp. 362–63).

For Lori Dunin Kelly (1983) Phelps's significance likewise lies in her iconoclastic view of women's experience. Kelly points out that where most of Phelps's contemporaries celebrated domestic life, Phelps detailed "the toll marriage exacted on a woman's personal growth and happiness."[29]

Contemporary male critics have thus far said little about Elizabeth Stuart Phelps. Her stories, unlike those of Mary Wilkins Freeman, Kate Chopin, and Sarah Orne Jewett, have not yet found their way into college anthologies. Whatever the final critical verdict, it is already clear, however, that Elizabeth Stuart Phelps occupies an important place in American letters because of her outspoken feminism at a point in time when women were expected to be silent partners.

NOTES

1. Elizabeth Stuart Phelps, "The Higher Claim," *Independent* 23 (October 5, 1871): 1.

2. Letter to John Greenleaf Whittier, October 17, 1871, Essex Institute, as quoted in Mary Angela Bennett, "Elizabeth Stuart Phelps" (diss., University of Pennsylvania, 1939), pp. 56–57.

3. Christine Stansell, "Woman: An Issue," *Massachusetts Review* 13 (1972): 244.

4. Elizabeth Stuart Phelps, *Chapters from a Life* (Boston: Houghton Mifflin, 1896), p. 15.

5. Ibid., pp. 156–57.

6. Elizabeth Stuart Phelps, "Women and Money," *Independent* 23 (August 14, 1871): 1; Elizabeth Stuart Phelps, "The True Woman," *Independent* 23 (October 19, 1871): 1.

7. Elizabeth Stuart Phelps, "What Shall They Do?" *Harper's New Monthly* 35 (September 1867): 519–23.

8. Elizabeth Stuart Phelps, *Austin Phelps* (New York: Scribner's, 1891), p. 87.

9. Elizabeth Stuart Phelps, *The Silent Partner and "The Tenth of January,"* Afterword by Mari Jo Buhle and Florence Howe (1871: rpt. Old Westbury, N.Y.: Feminist Press, 1983). All further references to this work will be indicated parenthetically within the text.

10. Carol Farley Kessler, *Elizabeth Stuart Phelps* (Boston: Twayne, 1982), p. 83.

11. Elizabeth Stuart Phelps, Historical Society of Pennsylvania, ms., April 1876.

12. Phelps, *Chapters from a Life*, pp. 92–93, 156.

13. As quoted in Kessler, *Elizabeth Stuart Phelps*, p. 127.

14. Ibid., pp. 125–26.

15. Rev. of *The Silent Partner*, *Literary World* 1 (April 1, 1871): 165–67.

16. Rev. of *The Silent Partner*, *Harper's New Monthly* 43 (June 1871): 300–301.

17. Bliss Perry, *A Study of Prose Fiction* (Cambridge, Mass.: Riverside Press, 1902), pp. 347–48.

18. Fred Lewis Pattee, *A History of American Literature Since 1870* (New York: Century, 1915), p. 223.

19. Fred Lewis Pattee, *Development of the American Short Story* (New York: Harper, 1923), p. 181.

20. Vernon Parrington, *Main Currents in American Thought* (New York: Harcourt, Brace, 1927–1930), p. 62.

21. John Macy, *American Writers on American Literature* (New York: Horace Liveright, 1931), p. 412.

22. Arthur Hobson Quinn, *American Fiction: An Historical and Critical Survey* (New York: Appleton-Century-Crofts, 1936), pp. 196, 203.

23. Van Wyck Brooks, *New England: Indian Summer 1865–1915* (New York: E. P. Dutton, 1940), p. 82.

24. Arthur Hobson Quinn, *The Literature of the American People* (New York: Appleton-Century-Crofts, 1951), p. 954.

25. Kessler, Preface, *Elizabeth Stuart Phelps*.

26. Christine Stansell, "Woman: An Issue," *Massachusetts Review* 13 (1972): 239.

27. Lee Edwards and Arlyn Diamond, Introduction, *American Voices, American Women* (New York: Avon, 1973), p. 13.

28. Kessler, Preface, *Elizabeth Stuart Phelps*.

29. Lori Dunin Kelly, *The Life and Works of Elizabeth Stuart Phelps: Victorian Feminist Writer* (Troy, N.Y.: Whitson, 1983), pp. 119–121.

4

Sisterhood and the Adamless Eden: Louisa May Alcott, *Work: A Story of Experience* (1873)

Louisa May Alcott was born in Germantown, Pennsylvania, on November 29, 1832. Her biographers agree that her life and work were shaped significantly by her observations of her parents' intensely complex and troubled relationship. Bronson Alcott was a philosopher immersed in transcendentalism, homeopathic medicine, and Socratic wisdom. He appears to have been more dedicated to his philosophic ideals than to his family, so that his long-suffering wife, Abba May, was left not only to rear their four daughters but to provide a living for her young family, who from time to time were forced to live on the charity of friends.

When Louisa was ten years old Abba May wrote of Bronson: "Wife, children and friends are less to him than the great ideas he is seeking to realize. How naturally man's sphere seems to be in the region of the head and woman's in the heart and affections."[1] The marriage nearly collapsed entirely when Bronson joined with his friend Charles Lane to create a new Eden at Fruitlands. Martha Saxton describes Abba at this time as an "embittered feminist" who frequently vented her feelings in her journal. "A woman may perform the most disinterested duties," she wrote, but she "lives neglected, dies forgotten." In contrast, "a man who never performed in his whole life one self-denying act, but who has accidental gifts of genius, is celebrated by his contemporaries, while his name and works live on from age to age."[2] Bronson and Abba talked of separation, and finally Bronson was forced to choose between Lane and Abba. Abba won, and Fruitlands' short, troubled life ended. But talk of the possibility of breaking up the marriage continued.

There was a clear need in the Alcott household for someone to play the traditional father role of breadwinner, and Abba looked to Louisa, who attempted to fulfill her mother's expectations by becoming housemaid, governess, teacher, seamstress, army nurse, lady's companion, and finally, celebrated author. In short, she explored the world of work open to a middle-class woman. Bronson, like Abba, thought of Louisa's role in the family as more male than female. When Louisa enlisted as an army nurse, he is reported to have told friends and acquaintances that "he was sending his only son to war."[3] Louisa seems to have accepted her parents' view on this subject, and according to Katherine Anthony, thought of herself as a boy.

Nonetheless, there is record of a love affair of some kind between Louisa and Ladislas Wisniewski, a young Polish musician whom she met in Vevey, Switzerland. Alcott's biographers differ in their views of the relationship. Katherine Anthony writes of a charming romance, while Madeline Stern indicates that Wisniewski was really interested in Louisa's traveling companion. Martha Saxton, on the other hand, claims that while Louisa loved Wisniewski, the relationship was based on language lessons and conversation. Since Wisniewski was eighteen and Alcott thirty-three, this last speculation seems reasonable. Another possible suitor has been suggested by Sarah Elbert (Diamant), who found a reference to a young doctor named John Winston in Louisa's journal. Whatever the full truth of either of these relationships, it seems safe to say that no man ever posed a serious threat to the spinsterhood Alcott apparently chose.

The relationship between Abba and Bronson must have demonstrated to Louisa that marriage was a risky business for a woman who had no vocation of her own and was therefore forced to depend on her husband for the sustenance of her family and herself. It was apparently not feminist ideology so much as the exigencies of life which forced Louisa to value female independence and to advance that notion in her fiction.

Another important early influence that undoubtedly contributed to Alcott's views on women was provided by the Reverend Theodore Parker. Alcott attended his services in Boston, and he is known to have helped her during a very troubled period in her life. In describing the characters in *Work*, Alcott wrote, "Christie's adventures are many of them my own; Mr. Power is Mr. Parker."[4] Parker was sympathetic to the plight of working women, and Alcott is believed to have become involved in that cause through his influence. Furthermore, Alcott appears to have adopted many of his ideas about women. He supported equality for women, specifically stating that women deserved voting rights and access to the professions of medicine, law, and theology. Nonetheless, he maintained that women should marry and give priority to the domestic sphere even while pursuing other interests.[5] Alcott's life and work frequently suggest that she believed Parker's ideas about women's capabilities and right to equality, but his ideas about the priorities of domesticity must have caused her concern. Her heroines, unlike Parker's model of an ideal woman, were, like herself, independent women, who for one reason or another were free of marital duties.

While Alcott was sympathetic to the aims of the women's rights movement, her direct participation was limited. She signed the Declaration of Principles in a public call to the first meeting of the New England Woman's Suffrage Association in 1868. In 1879, when Massachusetts gave women school tax and bond suffrage, she was the first woman to register to vote, and thereafter she made efforts to get other town women to do the same. She also attended the Woman's Congress in Syracuse and spoke in Concord on the causes of temperance and suffrage. In addition, she sent occasional letters to the *Woman's Journal*. Her interest in woman's suffrage was, however, secondary to her interest in woman's economic issues, and she is reported to have commented, "I am so busy just now proving 'woman's right to labor,' that I have no time to help prove 'woman's right to vote.' "[6]

Like other writers considered here, Louisa May Alcott made her chief contribution to feminism not through political action but through her literary work. She explored aspects of woman's role in a number of her books. If in life Alcott saw woman as underdog or victim, in her fiction she created other possibilities, namely, the dominant woman, the equal woman, and the independent woman who operates in a world which is essentially devoid of men.

Her recently discovered gothic tales, which she published under an androgynous pseudonym, A. M. Barnard, portray a number of powerful heroines. Especially memorable is Jean Muir, protagonist of "Behind a Mask; or, A Woman's Power." Jean Muir, a seemingly innocuous governess, succeeds through trickery in captivating all the men in the household in which she is employed. First the younger son, then the elder, and finally the middle-aged lord fall hopelessly in love with Jean, who has mysteriously persuaded them all that she is young and innocent, when, in fact, she is a middle-aged woman, experienced in the art of coquetry. In the end she marries Sir John, the head of the House of Coventry, thus gaining a title and an estate. Her power is so overwhelming that even when her dishonesty is revealed, Sir John refuses to listen to the accusations, begging only that the family accept his dear wife.

Since Alcott herself never achieved power over men, in her realistic autobiographical novels, *Little Women* and *Work*, her heroines must find an alternative way of finding happiness. In both novels women are separated from men by circumstances and find love and contentment with each other. In *Little Women* the father, who is serving in the war, is absent from the first part of the novel, leaving Marmee and the four girls to live happily in a pleasant matriarchy. This same theme is even more fully developed in *Work*, which ends with an autonomous community of women pledged to a common cause. The second half of *Little Women*, which was published two years after the first, is contrary to Alcott's original vision in that three of the girls marry. Alcott explained this conclusion in a letter to Sam May in which she wrote, "Publishers are very perverse and won't let authors have their own way so my little women must grow up and be married off in a very stupid style."[7]

A third possibility for a woman, aside from spinsterhood or marriage, is equal coexistence in an adrogynous society. This possibility is explored in a short story called "Cupid and Chow-Chow." The story is one of role reversal in which Cupid is portrayed as a rather effeminate boy, while Chow-Chow, his cousin, is a very independent girl. Like Louisa May Alcott herself, she was brought up "according to the new lights,—with contempt for dress and all frivolous pursuits, to make her hardy, independent, and quite above caring for such trifles as love, domestic life, or the feminine accomplishments we used to find so charming." But in the end the children decide "the fairest way is to cut it 'zactly in halves."[8] Thus, each sex becomes more like the other, and harmony is achieved.

If Alcott's stories inevitably end happily, her own life did not. Although she became famous and wealthy with the publication of *Little Women* in 1868, she continued to suffer bouts of depression which had plagued her through her life, and she complained often of loneliness and overwork. She died two days after Bronson of what was described as spinal meningitis or an apoplectic stroke. But according to Katherine Anthony, she was in a state of despair so intense that she was wasting away from sleeplessness and starvation.

WORK: A STORY OF EXPERIENCE

Work is a realistic autobiographical novel told in the third person by a narrator who, despite occasional authorial asides, maintains distance. As Alcott follows her protagonist's adventures, she recreates a woman's world not only through her woman-centered plot but through the images of cooking, baking, washing, dressing, and gossiping that constituted the predominant female lifestyle in the nineteenth century.

The opening scene immediately indicates the novel's message. Christie announces to Aunt Betsey that she is about to leave home to find her life's work. The message is communicated as Christie energetically kneads the dough that she and her aunt are molding into bread. Using images of baking that Aunt Betsey can readily grasp, Christie explains that she has yeast in her composition, so that if she stands in a corner fermenting, she will spoil and turn sour. Instead she must be kneaded into a wholesome loaf, and, therefore, she must leave.

If the imagery is domestic, the message is nonetheless, universal. *Work* may be viewed as Louisa May Alcott's version of *Pilgrim's Progress*. Not only are there specific references to that work in the novel, but there are important similarities in narrative structure. Christie, like Bunyan's Christian, after whom she is apparently named, embarks on life's pilgrimage in an effort to find her Celestial City. There are temptations to be avoided along the way and more than one Slough of Despond from which she must extricate herself, but with perseverance and luck she finds the right path. Christie's journey is, nonetheless, different from Christian's in at least two ways. Although she frequently hopes she can find salvation through God, hers is essentially a secular journey, and the Celestial City must be created on Earth. Moreover, both the pitfalls and the achievement are confined within the limits of possibility for a woman in nineteenth-century America.

Like Christian, Christie must leave her home and family to begin her difficult journey. Her desire for a better life seems to have been fed by an odd combination of feminist readings and fairy tales, both of which suggest possibilities for a young woman that far exceed the options offered by her present life on her uncle's farm. She reflects that if she stays, she could marry Joe Butterfield and become a household drudge, settle down to sour spinsterhood, or become a suicide.

Instead she announces to Aunt Betsey that there is going to be a "new Declaration of Independence."[9] The notion of a new Declaration of Independence was, of course, advanced at Seneca Falls, and the use of the term here suggests Christie's desire to assert her rights as a woman. She goes on to explain to her somewhat puzzled aunt that she must above all find independence, observing that had she been a boy, she would have been told to do so long ago. A little later she adds, "I'm not going to sit and wait for any man to give me independence, if I can earn it for myself" (p. 8). Thus at the outset it is made clear that Christie's intent is to reject the prevailing social mores.

Christie is at a loss, however, to define how a young woman is to achieve independence. The political statement at the Seneca Falls convention provided no guidelines for a young woman in a society that had not been created by and for women. Therefore, she can resort only to fairy tales. She announces that she will, "like the people in fairy tales, travel away into the world to seek my fortune" (p. 2).

Christie's first stop on her journey is a room of her own in a boarding house. She feels "delightfully independent" because she is freed from domestic chores, an unwanted farmer lover and the daily imprisonment of teaching in the local school (p. 16). Nonetheless, her options are limited. She decides to become a governess, a profession which is described as "the usual refuge for respectable girls who have a living to get" (p. 16). But she soon discovers that she is insufficiently skilled in the "ornamental branches of learning" (p. 16) and must, therefore, resort to becoming a housemaid.

At this point Christie's education begins in earnest, and the novel invites comparisons not only to *Pilgrim's Progress* but also to other works in American literature which develop the theme of a young protagonist's education and search for adventure. There is, for example, a parallel between Christie and two of the most celebrated characters in American literature, Huckleberry Finn and Ishmael. Eschewing formal education and rejecting expectations of their society, each undertakes a journey, the one on a raft, the other on a whaling ship. As outsiders they are able to study and learn from those they meet along the way. Just as Ishmael explains that "a whale-ship was my Yale College and my Harvard,"[10] so Christie might have suggested that her various jobs were also her university. Moreover, her desire to escape from home and seek adventure is as urgent and inevitable as that of Huck Finn or Ishmael.

In *Work*, as in *Moby Dick* and *Huckleberry Finn*, the socially rebellious protagonist learns a great deal through the loving companionship of a black friend. Christie's first important encounter is with Hepsey, a cook and former slave who is her co-worker and mentor in the Stuart household. When Christie complains about blacking Mr. Stuart's boots, Hepsey teaches her the lesson that guides the rest of her life, that work is not degradation, for it is through work that one attains freedom. Hepsey does not accompany Christie on her journey as does Jim in *Huckleberry Finn* or Queequeg in *Moby Dick*, but Hepsey's philosophy informs the rest of Christie's life.

In addition to providing a friend and mentor in Hepsey, Christie's job in the Stuart household provides her with the first of many opportunities to observe a part of the world she has not seen before. She is at first fascinated with the elegant ladies and gentlemen who frequent the Stuart home, but soon she complains that they are little more than trained canaries. Mrs. Stuart is a caricature of a rich woman who pretends to be artistic but in reality can find no purpose in life. She attempts to alleviate boredom by collecting water bugs and snakes in a glass globe and copying a Turner, which "was sold upside down and no one found it out" (pp. 17-18). Despite her aristocratic manner, she is rather dull, and when Christie is finally dismissed for accidentally setting fire to a curtain, she is glad to leave.

Christie soon finds work as an actress, and initially she is titillated by what she considers an enchanted world, but after three

years she is bored and disheartened. She seems finally to adopt the
prevailing opinion in the nineteenth century that acting was not a
respectable career. Worried that although she is becoming a good
actress, she is not becoming a good woman, she resolves to move
on.

Christie increases her knowledge of French and music sufficiently to secure a job as governess and once more is able to enter
the world of wealth and fashion. Again she becomes a critical ob-
server of woman's role. Her new employer, Mrs. Saltonstall, spends
her time in trivial amusements, namely, dressing, dining, driving,
dancing, skimming novels, and embroidering muslin. When she goes
to church, it is to exhibit her new bonnet and velvet prayer book.
Meanwhile she has a husband somewhere abroad who provides
money and leaves her to her own devices. She loves her children,
but only with the "love of a shallow heart" (p. 65). In the Saltonstall household, as in the Stuart home earlier, Christie finds her
employer sadly lacking as a role model. Mrs. Saltonstall is superficial and above all lacks what Christie comes to value as the greatest
human virtue, a loving heart.

As Mrs. Saltonstall's employee, Christie is afforded several opportunities to assess marriage as a possible career choice. Not only
does she observe Mrs. Saltonstall, but she eavesdrops on the con-
versations of her friends, who are assiduously hunting husbands.
She overhears one young woman explain: "You can do anything
you like with a husband a good deal older than yourself. He's happy
with his business, his club, and his dinner, and leaves you to do
what you please; just keep him comfortable, and he'll pay your
bills without much fuss" (p. 77). If the statement is callous, Christie herself is at least briefly persuaded of its logic. As long as women
were excluded from the most lucrative professions, marriage was
the obvious career choice for those who had the opportunity to
acquire a wealthy husband.

This opportunity is presented to Christie with the appearance of
Phillip Fletcher, Mrs. Saltonstall's somewhat dissolute but nonetheless wealthy brother. As Christie perceives Mr. Fletcher's interest in her, she begins to fantasize about a life of ease and pleasure,
and she resolves that if he proposes marriage, she will accept him.
She even considers that she might be morally justified in her choice
because she would have the opportunity to help Mr. Fletcher be-

come a better man, a role which was, as noted earlier, frequently expected of nineteenth-century women. But Christie in a discussion with Mr. Fletcher about *Jane Eyre* ultimately rejects the notion of woman as helpmate to a morally inferior man. She confesses that she likes Jane but dislikes Mr. Rochester because there is an unfair bargain in which Mr. Rochester gets the best of the deal. When Mr. Fletcher finally proposes, Christie breaks her earlier resolve to accept him and yield to a desire for money and comfort.

Forced to leave Mrs. Saltonstall's employ after her rejection of Mr. Fletcher, Christie finds work as a companion to Helen, a young woman who is dying of a hereditary mental illness. She befriends not only the dying woman but other family members, particularly Helen's younger sister, Bella, who becomes a lifelong friend. When Helen commits suicide Christie is so grieved that despite the family's willingness to have her remain, she decides to leave, taking with her what appears to be a fairly large gift of money. This she sends to Hepsey to buy "shares in the Underground Railroad" (p. 128). Like other women of her time imbued with a desire for independence, Christie maintains a commitment to helping blacks achieve freedom and a better life.

Her next job is as a seamstress, and in this capacity she meets Rachel, a co-worker, who is to become her closest friend. Rachel's and Christie's promises of love to one another may seem somewhat puzzling to a twentieth-century reader. According to historian Carroll Smith-Rosenberg, deep emotional ties such as those expressed by Rachel and Christie were abundant in America in the eighteenth and nineteenth centuries. The taboo that exists today did not, according to Smith-Rosenberg, exist in nineteenth-century American society.[11] In light of Smith-Rosenberg's thesis, the relationship between Christie and Rachel might be viewed not only as normal but as necessary and even inevitable. The close friendship between the two is, however, abruptly interrupted when Rachel is dismissed by her employer, who has discovered that Rachel had once run off with a lover. Christie immediately forgives Rachel and resigns in protest, but unwilling to cause her friend further harm, Rachel insists that she must go away alone. Christie is thus left lonely and bereft.

At this point she ponders the possibility of finding happiness through religion, but formal religion provides little comfort to her.

Christie seeks "sympathy and love" in religion, but she finds only "a God of wrath," who must be "adored like an idol" (p. 146). If piety in the traditional sense was an attribute of True Womanhood, as conceived by the purveyors of that term, dissatisfaction with traditional religious belief and practice was endemic among independent women. For Christie organized religion appears to be merely a manifestation of an oppressive society.

After parting with Rachel and failing to find solace in religion, Christie falls into a state of despair so intense that she contemplates suicide, as did Alcott at one time in her life. Christie's desire for death is described as a woman's "dreadful loneliness of heart, a hunger for home and friends worse than starvation, a bitter sense of wrong in being denied the tender ties, the pleasant duties, the sweet rewards that can make the humblest life happy; a rebellious protest against God, who when they cry for bread, seems to offer them a stone" (p. 150).

This longing for home and "tender ties" would seem to suggest that Christie might have been happier had she made the conventional choice of marriage and family. But the novel does not admit this possibility. While Christie feels a loss, she never considers returning to Aunt Betsey or her former suitor any more than Huck considers returning to Miss Watson and the Widow Douglas. Rather, a new home must be created. The dilemma for Christie, as for Huck, is to reconcile the need for love and the desire for freedom. At the moment when this seems beyond her grasp, help comes with the unexpected arrival of a loved one.

As Christie stands perched on the edge of a wharf looking into the gulf, she is miraculously rescued by Rachel, who appears at the penultimate moment. Rachel has been devoting her life to helping others and explains to Christie that personal salvation can be attained in this way. She then takes Christie to the home of the washerwoman, Mrs. Wilkins, who epitomizes all the virtues of an ideal mother. Through motherly love Christie will regain spiritual health.

Mrs. Wilkins also provides the religious understanding that Christie was unable to find in books and sermons. Using the imagery of a woman's daily chores, as Christie had done earlier, Mrs. Wilkins is able to reach Christie, as books and sermons could not. Mrs. Wilkins explains that "folks is very like clothes, and a sight has to be done to keep 'em clean" (p. 203). It is the minister, Mr. Thomas Power, who is entrusted with the "scrubbin" and "billin" (p. 203) to remove the stains. At Mrs. Wilkins's suggestion, Christie goes to Mr. Power's "free church" and is captivated by his sermon. Christie thus returns to religion outside the established church.

Shortly thereafter Mr. Power finds new work for Christie helping a Quaker lady, Mrs. Sterling, with the housework. Meanwhile she continues to attend Mr. Power's sermons, and the effect on her is reminiscent of Christian's ascent in *Pilgrim's Progress*: "Christie felt as if she was climbing up from a solitary valley, through mist and shadow toward a mountain top, where, though the way might be rough and strong winds blow, she would get a wider outlook over the broad earth, and be nearer the serene blue sky" (p. 213).

Working for Mr. Sterling marks the beginning of a new life for Christie because she soon falls in love with David Sterling, who Alcott's biographers seem to agree was modeled after Henry David Thoreau, a long-time friend of the Alcott family. Certainly there appears to be more of friendship than romance between the two. Thus, the only love affair that Alcott ever attempted to describe in some detail is hardly a love affair at all.

Once David and Christie decide to marry, however, the novel takes on a new dimension because it makes an attempt to define marriage as a contract between equal partners. This is in sharp contrast to other marriages that have been depicted earlier in the novel, all of which appear to be unsatisfactory compromises. The marriages of the rich, where the wife derives considerable material benefit, have already been mentioned. Two other marriages portrayed in the book appear to reflect Alcott's observations of her parents insofar as the wife, like Abba May, is the mainstay of the family, who provides moral support to the husband and nurturance to other family members, while the husband's role is negligible.

The first marriage presented in the novel is that of Aunt Betsey and Uncle Enos. As Christie looks at her kindly aunt and her gruff old husband, she concludes that Aunt Betsey made a bad bargain in exchanging girlish aspirations for a man without a soul. Later, in observing the marriage between Cynthia and Elisha Wilkins, Christie once again feels sympathetic to the wife, while she denigrates the husband, who is described as a "small, sallow, sickly looking man," about whom Mrs. Wilkins tells polite fibs. Nonetheless, Mrs. Wilkins endows her husband with her own virtues and intelligence and earns Christie's admiration for her devotion.

Christie's marriage to David is markedly different. When just before the marriage David enlists in the army, so does Christie. They agree to marry on the very day that David must depart to serve in the Union Army. Christie does not wear a bridal gown but an army uniform, which is the counterpart of her husband's clothing. This egalitarian marriage is, however, as ephemeral as one of Christie's favorite fairy tales. After the wedding day husband and wife part to serve in their different capacities, he as soldier, she as nurse. They meet occasionally during the war until the day that Christie is notified that David has been fatally wounded. Christie, now pregnant, rushes to David's side, and he dies in her arms. Thus Christie once again is independent, and Alcott never comes to grip with the issue of egalitarian marriage.

Christie is obliged to find her Celestial City in a community of women. The child she bears is a daughter, Pansy, who seems to fill the vacuum left by David. Together Christie and Pansy tend the garden that was David's legacy. They form a family unit with Mrs. Sterling and Rachel, who turns out to be none other than David's sister, who had been presumed dead. Thus Christie's family, like Alcott's own, becomes a matriarchal society of women.

Though content with her newly constituted family, Christie feels the need to reach out to the larger community. She goes to a meeting of working women where the wealthy ladies attempt to offer assistance to their downtrodden working-class sisters. But despite good will, the two classes are unable to bridge the gap until Christie, who through her experiences has gained an understanding of both classes, ascends the speaker's platform and makes a speech that creates unity of purpose. In the final pages of the novel she speculates that she has found a goal to "help lay the foundations of a new emancipation" (p. 431).

At the end Christie is pictured seated at a round table with those women who have had an impact on her life: Mrs. Wilkins, Hepsey, Rachel, Bella, and even little Pansy. Together they represent old and young, rich and poor, and black and white. Their goal is not very clearly defined. We know only that they are preparing for "the coming of the happy end" (p. 442). Mrs. Wilkins has just delivered a gift, which is a "lovely picture of Mr. Greatheart leading the fugitives from the City of Destruction" (p. 440). If the Celestial City is not yet attained in the novel, Christie seems at least certain about the correct path.

What remains odd about Alcott's Celestial City is that it is the exclusive domain of women. In her utopian world women find happiness together outside the world of men. Alcott's attempt to create a utopia in fiction echoes her father's attempt to create a utopia in life. Despite the enormous optimism with which the novel ends, Louisa's utopia seems as unrealistic as Bronson's. Each created a garden from which no new life would spring.

CRITICISM

During her own life Alcott was viewed mainly as a writer of juveniles, and her books were not seriously reviewed by the periodicals. After rejecting one of Alcott's early stories, James T. Fields, editor of the *Atlantic*, is reported to have told her father, "Tell Louisa to stick to her teaching; she can never write."[12] Thomas Wentworth Higginson was equally deprecating. In 1877 he wrote, "Her muse was domestic, simple and sociable: the instinct of art she never had."[13] Henry James, however, did not agree with the prevailing opinion. When he read Alcott's first novel, *Moods*, he wrote: "With the exception of two or three celebrated names, we know not, indeed to whom in this country unless to Miss Alcott, we are to look for a novel above the average."[14] High praise also came from G. K. Chesterton in an article that originally appeared in the *Nation* in 1907, in which he declared, "even from a masculine standpoint, the books are very good; and second that from a feminine standpoint they are so good that their admirers have really lost sight of their goodness." He goes on to say that he feels like "the male intruder" in a "feminine world" but concludes that it is "a very interesting world."[15] Chesterton hit on a very important fact, namely, that Alcott was writing from a feminine vantage point for a female audience, and this fact may explain why her work seemed to elude well-respected male critics, for whom it evidently held little interest.

After Chesterton criticism of Alcott in the first half of the twentieth century either ignored or deprecated Alcott's work. In 1915 Fred Pattee dismissed *Little Women* as one of many novels produced

during the "feeblest period in American fiction."[16] Thomas Beer
(1926) called Alcott's work "moral pap for the young," and Van
Wyck Brooks (1940) ignored her books entirely but, nonetheless,
managed to give Alcott high praise for being "a strong-minded ad-
venturess."[17] Alexander Cowie (1948) and Arthur Hobson Quinn
(1951) were impressed with Alcott's sales but gave little consideration to the reasons for her popularity. Cowie speculated only that
Alcott's juveniles were "among the best domestic stories of the period."[18] These curt dismissals of Alcott's large body of fiction raises
questions about whether the critics really read the books or simply
read each other.

After half a century of neglect, interest in Alcott has increased
in recent decades, probably because of rising concern with women
writers as well as a more eclectic approach to literary criticism.
Writing in the *New York Times Book Review* (1964), Brigid Brophy
described the experience of rereading *Little Women* and *Good Women*:
"Having re-read them, dried my eyes and blown my nose . . . I
resolved that the only honourable course was to come out into the
open and admit that the dreadful books are masterpieces."[19] Rarely
since William Dean Howells had critics admitted to crying over
books, but there seems to be an admission here that sentiment is
not necessarily sentimentality and that even where novels do not
lend themselves to scholarly exegesis, they may, in fact, be very
good novels.

Literary criticism in the 1970s and 1980s suggests that Alcott's
work is not only serious but meaningful in ways that had previously been ignored. Madeline Stern (1975) writes of Alcott's gothic
tales, "These gory gruesome novelties were and still are extremely
good: well-paced, suspenseful, skillfully executed, and peopled with
characters of flesh and blood."[20]

Not surprisingly, most of the criticism has focused on Alcott's
most popular novel, *Little Women*. Rejecting the view that *Little
Women* is merely a sentimental juvenile novel, feminist critics have
looked for the special attributes that have made the work endure.
Madelon Bedell (1983) suggests that *Little Women* has the qualities
of a myth or legend and may even be "*the* American female myth,"
tracing the passage from childhood to girl to woman. She concludes that the general reader perceives this universality that seems

to have eluded most of the critics.[21] Nina Auerbach (1983) also acknowledges *Little Women*'s "perennial appeal" and "power."[22]

Looking directly at feminism itself, critics have advanced a variety of opinions. Patricia Meyer Spacks (1972) concludes that *Little Women* is anti-feminist because it is "a textbook example of damaging assumptions about the nature of the female and of the way a girl learns to be charming because she's not allowed to be intelligent or inventive."[23] In contrast to Spacks, both Sarah Elbert (Diamant) (1974) and Joy A. Marsella (1983) see Alcott as a "domestic feminist," a term which Elbert defines as an "outgrowth of both the domestic reform movement and the woman's rights movement."[24] Sandra Gilbert and Susan Gubar (1979), like Spacks, are concerned with Alcott's depiction of masculine and feminine roles, but they feel that far from advocating female submission, Alcott shows its high cost.[25]

Critical comment on *Work* is limited. On its first publication the reviews were discouraging. The *Lakeside Monthly* called the book "an immoderate apotheosis of Madame Work" and objected to its treatment of the subject of "Negro rights" as an outdated issue since the abolition of slavery.[26] *Harper's New Monthly* was equally disparaging in indicating that interest in the book would be based not on its merits but merely on its author's reputation.[27] In London the *Athenaeum* seemed to have missed the point entirely, complaining that Christie does not live "happy ever after."[28]

After a period of long neglect, *Work* has, however, captured the interest of contemporary critics, who have underscored its contribution to our understanding of its author and of women's history. Sarah Elbert (1977) considers that *Work* deserves to be read as "historical document and minor literary achievement." She also sees it as significant in establishing "the commonality of our daily struggle with those of our mothers and grandmothers."[29] Ellen Moers (1977) calls *Work* a "most interesting" and "oddly modern" novel, while Nina Auerbach (1983) sees in *Work* an attempt "to resolve the conflict between the surging emotion and creativity of the female community and the 'normal' tenderness and sacrifices of patriarchal marriage."[30]

No one as yet has attempted to place *Work* in the larger context of American literature—male and female—or to analyze its literary qualities. As a novel which at least in part is about female rebellion against the social norms, *Work* needs to be considered along with the paradigmatic male novels in which the hero rejects his society. Also, attention should be paid to Alcott's use of feminine imagery to describe a woman's world.

The publication of a college edition of *Work* in 1977 as well as two new college editions of *Little Women* in 1983 attest to a new interest in Louisa May Alcott. Thus it is clear that she is no longer being regarded as merely a writer of juveniles. Nonetheless, her place in American literature has yet to be established.

NOTES

1. Abigail Alcott's journal, July 21, 1842, Houghton Library, Harvard University, as quoted in Martha Saxton, *Louisa May: A Modern Biography of Louisa May Alcott* (Boston: Houghton Mifflin, 1977), p. 130.

2. Abigail Alcott's journal, August 1843, as quoted in Saxton, *Louisa May*, p. 143.

3. Katherine Anthony, *Louisa May Alcott* (1938, rpt. Westport, Conn.: Greenwood Press, 1977), p. 120.

4. See Ednah Cheney, *Louisa May Alcott, Her Life, Letters, and Journals* (Boston: Roberts Bros., 1897), p. 265.

5. Theodore Parker's Sermon (1853), "The Public Function of Woman," rpt. in Theodore Parker, *Sins and Safeguards of Society*, Vol. 4 (Boston: American Unitarian Association, 1907–1913), p. 178.

6. Anthony, *Louisa May Alcott*, p. 263.

7. As quoted in Madeline Stern, *Louisa May Alcott* (Norman: University of Oklahoma Press, 1950), pp. 189–90.

8. Louisa May Alcott, *Aunt Jo's Scrapbook*, Vol. 3 (Boston: Roberts Bros., 1896), pp. 7, 39.

9. Louisa May Alcott, *Work: A Story of Experience* (1873, rpt. New York: Schocken, 1977), p. 3. All further references to this work will be indicated parenthetically within the text.

10. Herman Melville, *Moby Dick* (1851, rpt. New York: Modern Library, 1930), p. 159.

11. "The Female World of Love and Ritual: Relations Between Women in Nineteenth-Century America," in *The Signs Reader: Women, Gender and Scholarship*, ed. Elizabeth Abel and Emily K. Abel (Chicago: University of Chicago Press, 1983), pp. 53–54.

12. As quoted in Anthony, *Louisa May Alcott*, p. 118.

13. Thomas Wentworth Higginson, *Short Studies of American Authors* (1877, rpt. New York: Longmans, 1966), pp. 66–67.

14. As quoted in Anthony, *Louisa May Alcott*, p. 177.

15. G. K. Chesterton, "Louisa Alcott," in *A Handful of Authors: Essays on Books and Writers* (1953; New York: Kraus, 1969), pp. 166–67.

16. Fred Lewis Pattee, *A History of American Literature Since 1870* (New York: Cooper Square, 1915), p. 63.

17. Thomas Beer, *The Mauve Decade: American Life at the End of the Century* (Garden City, N.Y.: Garden City Publishing, 1926), p. 26; Van Wyck Brooks, *New England: Indian Summer, 1865–1915* (New York: E. P. Dutton, 1940), p. 64.

18. Alexander Cowie, *The Rise of the American Novel* (New York: American Book, 1948), p. 821, note 71.

19. Brigid Brophy, "Sentimentality and Louisa May Alcott," *New York Times Book Review*, December 1964, rpt. in *Don't Never Forget: Collected Views and Reviews* (New York: Holt, Rinehart, 1966), p. 114.

20. Madeline Stern, Introduction, *Behind a Mask: The Unknown Thrillers of Louisa May Alcott* (New York: William Morrow, 1975), pp. vii–viii.

21. Madelon Bedell, Introduction, *Little Women*, by Louisa May Alcott (1868–1869, rpt. New York: Modern Library, 1983), p. xi.

22. Nina Auerbach, Afterword, *Little Women*, by Louisa May Alcott (New York: Bantam, 1983), p. 461.

23. Patricia Meyer Spacks, *The Female Imagination* (New York: Avon, 1972), p. 12.

24. Sarah Elbert (Diamant), "Louisa May Alcott and the Woman Problem," diss. Cornell University, 1974, p. 17; Joy A. Marsella, *The Promise of Destiny: Children and Women in the Short Stories of Louisa May Alcott* (Westport, Conn.: Greenwood Press, 1983), pp. 99–103.

25. Sandra Gilbert and Susan Gubar, *The Madwoman in the Attic: The Woman Writer and the Nineteenth-Century Literary Imagination* (New Haven: Yale University Press, 1979), p. 483.

26. Rev. of *Work: A Story of Experience*, *Lakeside Monthly* 10 (September 1873): 246–49, rpt. in *Critical Essays on Louisa May Alcott*, ed. Madeline Stern (Boston: G. K. Hall, 1984), pp. 187, 189.

27. Rev. of *Work: A Story of Experience*, *Harper's New Monthly Magazine* 47 (September 1873): 614–15.

28. Rev. of *Work: A Story of Experience*, *Athenaeum* (London), 62 (July 26, 1973), 111, rpt. in Madeline Stern, *Critical Essays on Louisa May Alcott*, p. 185.

29. Sarah Elbert, Introduction, *Work: A Story of Experience* (1873, rpt. New York: Schocken, 1977), p. xii.

30. Ellen Moers, *Literary Women* (Garden City, N.Y.: Anchor, 1977), pp. 131, 133; Auerbach, Afterword, *Little Women*, p. 23.

5

The Professional Woman and an Independent Life: Sarah Orne Jewett, *A Country Doctor* (1884)

Sarah Orne Jewett was born September 3, 1849, in South Berwick, Maine, to Theodore Herman Jewett and Caroline Frances Perry Jewett. Theodore Jewett was a well-respected country doctor. The family was prosperous, and Sarah Orne Jewett enjoyed a life of far greater ease and luxury than that which she generally depicted in her stories of the farmers and seamen of South Berwick.

The aspect of her biography most significant here is her adoration of her father. Because of ill health as a child, Jewett did not attend school regularly. Her mentor was her own father, with whom she often traveled as he made his rounds through the farms in South Berwick and neighboring areas. In her dedication to one collection of stories she wrote: "To T.H.J./My dear father; my dear friend;/The best and wisest man I ever knew/Who taught me many lessons and showed me many things/As we went together along the Country By-Ways."[1] When her father died she confessed to a long-time friend, "I don't know how I can live without him."[2]

More than any prose statement, however, her autobiographical novel, *A Country Doctor*, details Jewett's love and admiration. Like Nan, the little girl in *A Country Doctor*, Jewett felt her most valuable childhood experiences were the days spent at the side of the doctor while he made his rounds. She once wrote to Thomas Bailey Aldrich, "I felt sometimes as if I were Nan in the 'Country Doctor,' but usually like my own self who was being constantly reminded of very dear old days when I would drive about with Father, over the hills and down the river roads."[3]

In the novel Nan decides to become a doctor like her guardian, but Jewett chose writing instead. Nonetheless, there are obvious parallels in the choice. Like Nan, Jewett rejected what she perceived as the wife's role for an independent life, a life more like that of a man of her generation. Her negative view of the role of wife is documented in both her life and her fiction. Her biographers find no indication of a romance with a man, and F. O. Matthiessen asserts that she most assuredly felt that marriage would interfere with her dreams for herself.[4]

Certainly her fiction suggests that above all a woman must find happiness in her independence. In a story called "Tom's Husband," she described the wife, Mary, as "too independent and self-reliant for a wife." Indeed, Mary is viewed as needing a wife more than a husband. In order to solve their difficulties, the couple in the story decide to change roles, but the role change only highlights for the husband the inadequacies of a woman's life. He realizes that in merging his life in his wife's, he is sharing the experience of most married women, which he comes to regard as "disappointing" and "ignominious."[5]

A similar fear of being submerged in another's life is articulated in Jewett's best-known story, "A White Heron." In that story Sylvia, a young girl, must decide whether or not to tell a handsome hunter the whereabouts of a white heron. Sylvia is torn between her love for the hunter and her desire to save the heron. Although the hunter can make Sylvia and her grandmother rich, and although he himself is a worthy love object, Sylvia decides to keep her secret and exercise her independence. The story ends somewhat cryptically with the statement: "Dear loyalty, that suffered a sharp pang as the guest went away disappointed later in the day that could have served and followed him as a dog loves." The suggestion here that the love of a woman for a man is somehow like that of a dog is not developed in the story, but Sylvia's fear is very like that of Nan in *A Country Doctor*, who likewise decides to follow her own heart rather than serve and follow presumably "as a dog loves."

Whether or not Jewett herself feared being submerged in a man, as several of her protagonists do, is unclear. We know only that throughout her life her closest friends were women rather than men. Diary entries when she was a young girl indicate extremely close friendships with several girls. And the most important relationship of her adult life was with Annie Fields, the widow of James T. Fields. Jewett enjoyed the company of wealthy Boston society with Annie during the six months she lived with her either in Boston or Manchester each year. Her biographers speak of the love and devotion between the two women, but the question of whether the relationship was lesbian remains unsettled.

Whatever Jewett's sexual predilections, her fiction makes it clear that her interest was in women's lives. Throughout her pages are independent women who find emotional support from one another in a world where men are often excluded or relegated to supporting roles. The exception is Dr. Leslie in *A Country Doctor*, whom Nan loves as unequivocally as Jewett loved her own father.

When Sarah Orne Jewett died in 1909 after a long illness caused when she received spinal injuries as a result of being thrown from a carriage, she left four novels and a large body of short fiction.

A COUNTRY DOCTOR

Originally published in 1884, *A Country Doctor* remains a surprisingly modern novel in that it explores a number of issues which have been raised by feminists in recent years. Through her heroine, Nan (Anna) Prince, Sarah Orne Jewett expresses deeply felt convictions about the nature of woman and her role in marriage, the professions, and the family.

Jewett preferred *A Country Doctor* to all her other works, probably because she projected her own thoughts, dreams, aspirations, and conflicts onto her young protagonist, Nan. Thus the novel is autobiographical on two levels—both the realistic and external and the psychological and internal.

The father-daughter relationship becomes the springboard for the novel's plot, which involves a decision Nan must make—to assume a traditional wife's role, as her mother had attempted to do, or to pursue a medical career as both her guardian and her deceased father had done. A number of critics have compared this choice to the choice Jewett herself had to make when she chose to become a professional writer.[6]

Moreover, descriptions of Nan in the novel often seem to be descriptions of Sarah Orne Jewett. In discussing Nan, her grandmother comments that although she is "lovin'-hearted," she's a "piece of mischief," who is "wild as ever" (p. 71). These words are echoed in Matthiessen's comments about Jewett: "she was forever getting tangled up in her emotions, and then bursting out of the house and riding too fast for good manners and then having to try all over again not to let her boyishness make her rude and unladylike."[7]

Jewett's descriptions of herself are sometimes hard to distinguish from her descriptions of Nan. She uses the image of a plant to describe both her own development and Nan's. Of herself she wrote, "I wish I grew in three or four smooth useful branches instead of starting out here, there, and everywhere and doing nothing of any account at any point."[8] Dr. Leslie, observing that Nan has grown like a plant, also notes that such growth is unruly, but far from wishing that Nan were different, he is pleased that she has not been "clipped back or forced in any unnatural direction" (p. 102).

The young Sarah Orne Jewett disliked housekeeping and pondered what she would do with her life if she rejected the traditional woman's role. Jewett apologized about shutting herself up half of every day when there were things to be done in the house, but, nonetheless, she complained, "I have nothing to do with the housekeeping or anything of that kind, but there are bits of work waiting all the time that use up my days."[9] Similarly, Nan is described as "restless and dissatisfied." And Dr. Leslie notes "how impossible it was for her to content herself with following the round of household duties which were supposed to content young women of her age and status" (p. 162). It remains then for Nan, like Jewett, to identify the gift which will allow her to rise above the commonplace.

In justifying Sarah/Nan's choice, Jewett focuses on some of the key issues debated in late nineteenth-century America as women began to move out of the domestic world and into the larger world of industry and the professions. Of central concern in the debate were theories on women's nature, which Jewett undoubtedly read about in the monthlies and perhaps also found in her father's medical books. Josephine Donovan has recently suggested that it is likely that Jewett was familiar with Krafft-Ebings's *Psychopathia Sexualis*, published in Germany in 1882 and in this country in 1886, in which he argued against women's choice of masculine vocations as unnatural and asserted that what was natural for women was passivity.

It is in the context of the running debate on women's nature that we can best understand the lengthy arguments in *A Country Doctor* on what is natural and unnatural for women. In discussing Nan's future, Dr. Leslie explains that she must continue to work with nature and not against it, whether the work she chooses be "man's work" or "woman's work." [10]

Nan herself justifies her choice to become a doctor on the grounds that it would allow her to make the best possible use of God's gifts. Later, in reviewing the life options open to men and women, Nan speculates that God would not have given the same talents to both sexes if what were right for men were wrong for women.

In contrast to Nan is her mother, who, though she died when Nan was a baby, exercises a lifelong influence on her daughter. Dr. Leslie notes "the mother's nature in her daughter; a restless, impatient miserable urging for The Great Something Else" (p. 171). But Nan's mother's nature was thwarted when she married and attempted to live up to the expectations of her husband's relatives. As a result she became an alcoholic and a drifter, unable to help herself or anyone else.

The point is that for Jewett the literature about women's nature is wrong. In fact, women, like men, must follow their inner yearnings and perform life roles that are suitable to the individual, regardless of gender.

Moreover, while Jewett acknowledges the possibility that self-realization may be achieved by some women in domesticity, in fact, the novel demonstrates something else. Paraded before us are a number of female characters whose lives signify nothing but frivolity, frustration, or bored acceptance. Having lost her young lover when a girl, Nan's aunt, Miss Anna Prince, devotes herself to "tea parties" and what Nan sees as an "apparently fruitless society" (p. 231). Miss Prince's friend, Miss Fraley, is an aging obedient daughter, who admits sadly that she often feels as if she were not accomplishing anything. Similarly, Dr. Leslie's friend and neighbor, Mrs. Graham, watches life from a seat by the window and complains of the boredom of her days. And while Nan's grandmother, Mrs. Thacher, the Dyer sisters, who appear briefly in the novel's opening pages, and Dr. Leslie's housekeeper, Marilla, are all apparently content with their housewifely chores, Nan is unable to see much to emulate in their lives.

Instead Nan craves options which are generally considered the sole prerogatives of men. At one point, when she is thinking about her medical career, she laments, "If a young man plans the same course, everything conspires to help him and forward him. . . . " In contrast she finds no interest or encouragement from school or society (pp. 192–93). This argument would later be more fully articulated in Charlotte Perkins Gilman's *Women and Economics*, but if Jewett did not attempt to construct a theory of economics, she felt the same sense of injustice which gave rise to Gilman's impassioned political outcry. Women could not be happy as long as they were expected to be naturally inclined only to the routines of domestic life.

Furthermore, according to Jewett, it is not only women who suffer from arbitrary social constraints. Just as Nan finds a woman's presumed role uncongenial, the novel suggests that a man may also find his role unsuitable, or to use the jargon of the day, unnatural. When George Gerry courts Nan in the final scenes of the novel, he is frequently frustrated or bewildered in his attempts to fit the male prototype. As Nan efficiently sets the shoulder of a local farmer, George looks on chagrined, feeling "weak and womanish" and wishing that he could "play the doctor" (p. 266). George wants desperately to be Nan's champion, defending her against harm in the best chivalrous tradition, but he realizes that Nan could "get on capitally well without him" (p. 298). Thus Jewett refutes Krafft-Ebings's theories about men as well as women. There seems to be nothing natural about nineteenth-century sex roles.

If the sexual politics of *A Country Doctor* are of particular interest here, it would be misleading to present only that aspect of the book. With its scenes of rural life lovingly depicted, the novel, like most of Jewett's work, is notable for its realism and contributes to Jewett's reputation as an outstanding regional writer of New England. Village and seaport come alive as Jewett fleshes in the details of the lives of the farmers, sea captains, and lonely spinsters who people the towns she knew. And yet to view the novel as merely another example of literary realism is also too limited an approach. *A Country Doctor* fascinates in part because of its exploration of psychosexual concerns, which are presented through the medium of the fairy tale that weaves in and out of the realistic details of the plot.

The novel opens with a mysterious scene in which a young woman is depicted carrying a child through a dark and lonely landscape. The woman, identified only as "the lonely woman," takes the child to the river bank for a reason as yet unknown. The child cries, "No, no!" and the woman turns back into the neighboring grave-yard and proceeds at a rapid pace to a house, where she drops the child and collapses at the doorway. The child turns out to be Nan, and the woman is her mother, Adeline Prince, who dies soon thereafter, leaving Nan in the care of her grandmother. Kindly Mrs. Thacher raises Nan until she feels she is too old, and thereafter entrusts her care to Dr. Leslie. These events and the main story line that follows suggest a number of fairy tale motifs.

Nan's surname, "Prince," was probably not a random choice. The character of Nan closely parallels both the prince and princess of the fairy tale genre. Like many a fairy tale princess, she was orphaned when very young and raised by surrogates—her grand-mother and Dr. Leslie, whose wife had died long ago and who has no children. Thus Nan becomes the sole love object. Bruno Bettel-heim finds the paradigm for such a relationship in the earliest ver-sion of "Cinderella," which portrays a widowed prince who loves his daughter deeply and in turn is loved by her in a classic ocdipal situation.[11]

The fairy tale model also sheds light on the role of Nan's mother. As the novel progresses we learn that her reason for going to the river bank, as detailed in the opening scene, was to drown herself and her child. Why the unhappy woman wanted to kill not only herself but Nan is never revealed. We can only surmise that her motives are attributable to what are later described as "the evil gifts that had been buried with her" (p. 350). But what are we to make of this oblique reference to "evil gifts"? Once more the fairy tale may provide a possible answer. Fairy tales abound with evil step-mothers, who often have murderous thoughts about their daugh-ters, signifying the oedipal rivalry between mother and daughter. In *A Country Doctor*, as in fairy tales, the mother contemplates kill-ing the daughter, but in the end it is she who dies.

Eliminating the evil mother is only a partial solution. Since a child requires a mother's nurturance, the fairy tale provides a beneficent replacement, such as the fairy godmother in "Cinderella." In *A Country Doctor* the good mother prototype is realized in the character of Anna Prince, the sister of Nan's deceased father. Nan and her aunt bear the same given name; the replication of a name usually signifies a mother-daughter relationship rather than that of an aunt and niece. But more important, Nan's childhood dreams about her aunt indicate that she was conceived as a mother figure who would fill the place vacated in Nan's life. When she thought about her unknown aunt, Nan dreamed that "any day a carriage drawn by prancing black horses might be seen turning up the lane, and that a lovely lady might alight and claim her as her only niece." As time passed, "the dream of her had been growing longer and more charming until she seemed fit for a queen and her unknown house a palace" (pp. 65–66). In other words Nan longed to be united with a woman who would claim her and presumably provide her with the benefits of her exalted position as queen. In effect Nan would thereby become a princess.

As long as Nan was still a child, Miss Prince appeared only in dreams, but when she finally became a young woman of marriageable age and well beyond the phase of oedipal attachment, she left the doctor to visit the aunt who had so often filled her thoughts. Not only did Miss Prince happily claim her, as Nan had dreamed, but she soon performed the role of fairy godmother in introducing Nan to an ideal young man, whom she hoped Nan would marry. This young man, George Gerry, had the essential qualities of the handsome prince. Not only was he physically attractive, but he was Miss Prince's heir, and he wanted above all to make Nan his wife. Like all fairy tale heroes, he also longed to "rush into the field as Nan's champion" (p. 249). Nan had only to accept him and live happily ever after.

At this point, however, the novel breaks with fairy tale tradition, which assumes that a woman will find happiness in assuming her appropriate sex role as wife. But Nan's professional goals were identical with those of both her natural father and her surrogate father, suggesting her identification with a male rather than a female role. Sarah/Nan seemed painfully aware of the anomaly. At crucial points in the novel Nan is pictured literally following her mother's footsteps, but each time she turns away. One day during that period in her life when Nan is uncertain about her career choice, she decides to alleviate her anxiety by having "a good run." She returns to the old playground, unaware that she has been following her mother's footsteps, and there in the playground she makes the decision about her life. She realizes that she can follow her mother's footsteps just so far, because her destination is different. She decides to study medicine like her father and Dr. Leslie, for her mother's footsteps lead to spiritual death. This is metaphorically suggested in the final pages of the novel when Nan once again gravitates to the same place—the river uplands where her story began—and she thinks with a shudder of the footprints which had led to the brink of the river and then turned back. Instead Nan joyously decides to follow the male path. The traditional fairy tale comes to a conclusion which the nineteenth-century heroine rejects. The novel suggests that to live happily ever after, Nan must become the prince rather than the princess. Perhaps in the end Nan's surname signifies just that.

At the novel's conclusion Jewett is careful to point out that Nan's choice need not necessarily be emulated by other women. She acknowledges that most men and women will happily accept the "high duties and helps of married life" (pp. 336–37). What is important is to have options. Sarah Orne Jewett's answer to the Woman Question in her own life and in Nan's was simply to use the gift which she felt was bestowed by God, even if it meant sacrificing or compromising other aspects of life.

CRITICISM

In her own time Sarah Orne Jewett was generally well received by the critical establishment. William James wrote to her of the "exquisite pleasure" he had in reading *The Country of the Pointed Firs*. And Kipling exulted on reading that work, "It's immense—it is the very life." [12] John Greenleaf Whittier in a letter thanked Jewett for "thy admirable book, 'Deephaven,' " which he noted he was reading for the third time. [13]

Jewett was particularly admired by several women writers of her own and subsequent generations. Mary Wilkins Freeman enthusiastically praised her in a letter in which she stated, "I never wrote any story equal to your 'White Heron.' I don't think I ever read a short story, unless I except Tolstoy's 'Two Deaths,' that so appealed to me."[14] And Kate Chopin considered Jewett a mentor from whom she could study technique.[15] But the greatest compliment came from Willa Cather, who stated, "If I were asked to name the American books which have the possibility of a long, long life I would say at once, 'The Scarlet Letter,' 'Huckleberry Finn,' and 'The Country of the Pointed Firs.' "[16]

Although most of the reviewers offered praise for Jewett's work, there was occasional dissent. The *New York Times* wrote of *Deephaven*, "It is by some mistake that it got into print at all." And *Literary World* complained that *Country By-Ways* indulged in "little preachments." But the dissenters were few among the many who considered Jewett an important new talent. The *Saturday Review* praised her "brief and graceful stories," while *Harper's* called the stories "pure without prudery." The *Critic* rejoiced that every publication of a new volume was "a red letter day in the annals of New England story writing."[17] And Horace Scudder, writing in the *Atlantic Monthly*, praised Jewett's "geniune gift."[18] Edward Garnett in *Academy and Literature* called her "a writer who can be rated second only to Hawthorne in her interpretation of the spirit of New England soil,"[19] while Charles Miner Thompson, in an extended piece in the *Atlantic Monthly*, admired her for telling "the absolute truth about New England."[20]

In the decades that followed Jewett's death, critics were mixed in their responses. Several continued to praise her works for their beauty and verisimilitude, but others saw her as a minor talent, largely because of what they perceived as a very limited subject matter. Henry James in 1915 called Jewett

mistress of an art of fiction all her own, even though of minor compass, and surpassed only by Hawthorne, as producer of the most finished and penetrating of the numerous short stories that have the domestic life of New England for their general and their doubtless somewhat lean subject.[21]

In the years between 1920 and 1940, however, Jewett often fell victim to what Mary Ellman has recently called "phallic criticism," by which she means male literary criticism which emphasizes the femininity of the writer and ignores or denigrates the work.[22] Even where the criticism is not derogatory, such criticism often suggests that women's writing is outside the canon of real art. She claims that a characteristic of such criticism is the use of stereotypical adjectives to describe women's writing.

Among the following critical comments, several could undoubtedly qualify as "phallic criticism" as defined by Ellman. Fred Lewis Pattee (1923) praised Jewett for writing "sketches that are patrician in their fastidious beauty."[23] Like other critics who use such generalizations, Pattee gives no examples, but the implication is that Jewett's stories are composed of the perfume and lace that adorned ladies' scrapbooks of the time.

Vernon L. Parrington (1927–1930) condescendingly suggests, "Her realism—if one may use the word—was as dainty and refined as her own manners—bleached out to a fine maidenly purity."[24] Parrington never explains the phrase "fine maidenly purity." Certainly the evidence from both Jewett's life and work as discussed here suggests that she was fully aware of human passion in its many forms.

Matthiessen (1929) ranked Jewett as one of America's two principal women writers, the other being Emily Dickinson, but it is unclear where he placed her in the canon of American literature. To be a woman writer is obviously not the same as being a writer, a designation apparently reserved for men.

The anthologies of the 1930s were even less appreciative of Jewett's work. Ludwig Lewisohn (1932) complained of Sarah Orne Jewett and Mary Wilkins Freeman that their view was too limited, and the society they depicted was "the least fruitful that American artists sought to treat."[25] Granville Hicks's views (1933) provide the most marked examples of "phallic criticism." He wrote: "There is . . . nothing that we can admire her for except those delicate powers of perception that under favorable circumstances she could exercise so fruitfully. In other respects she was merely a New England old maid . . . who believed in piety, progress and propriety."[26] Again Jewett's work as discussed here belies the generalizations, which remain unsupported. The term "old maid" is not only denigrating but peculiarly sexist in that the marital status of male writers is seldom if ever a reason for pejorative comment.

Jewett fared somewhat better in the anthologies of the 1940s. Van Wyck Brooks (1940) maintained, "No one since Hawthorne has pictured this New England world with such exquisite freshness of feeling."[27] And Carlos Baker (1948) acknowledged *The Country of the Pointed Firs* as "the best piece of regional fiction to have come out of nineteenth-century America," and added that "her stories were works of art, and of a high order."[28]

By the 1950s two full-length works on Sarah Orne Jewett appeared: A. M. Buchan's *"Our Dear Sarah": An Essay on Sarah Orne Jewett* (1953) and Richard Cary's edition of her letters (1956). Buchan echoed those before him who found a femininity in the work, but unlike most of the others, he viewed this femininity as an asset more than a liability: "She creates not like a man, subduing the objects of the earth to his arrogant purpose and regarding them vaingloriously, but like a woman, guarding and perpetuating within herself the essential human values."[29]

Since the 1960s there has been a great revival of scholarly interest in Jewett. Several full-length books have appeared, as well as a number of articles, most of which deal principally with *The Country of the Pointed Firs*. Richard Cary (1962), in particular, has objected to the categorization of Jewett as a woman author and by implication therefore a lesser writer. Taking Matthiessen to task for placing Sarah Orne Jewett with Emily Dickinson as the best female American authors, Cary wrote, "If so exalted a position is warranted credit must also go to the insistent individuality, the copious heart, the innate understanding, and the unsuffered sensibility that informs every line of her mature writings."[30]

In the introduction to a book of selected fiction by Sarah Orne Jewett and Mary Wilkins Freeman, Barbara Solomon (1979) attributes a revived interest in both writers to a greater appreciation of regionalism and to the modernity of the roles dramatized, which has been of special interest to feminists.[31] Also noting the innovative quality of Jewett's work, Josephine Donovan (1980) suggests that Jewett was part of a new movement in American letters, marked by a departure from the romance and sentimentalism that characterized fiction of an earlier generation.[32]

Criticism devoted exclusively to *A Country Doctor* is sparse, but what does exist is mainly though not entirely favorable. On the novel's initial publication the review in the *Atlantic Monthly* (1884) called it "an interesting book," "a wise book," and "a graceful book." The reviewer goes on to describe it as "feminine" in its treatment,

a term which is never explained, but he exults, "Heaven be praised
for a handling of the theme which is absolutely free from hysterics
and regards men and women in a wholesome, honest fashion."[33]
This appears to be a veiled reference to the feminism in the novel,
which is apparently accepted because it is perceived as rational rather
than angry. The *Critic*, however, complained, "The life is so still
. . . it may be called photographic." And the *Nation* wondered
whether it was a novel at all.[34]

Only one contemporary critic, a Frenchwoman who used the
pen name Th. Bentzon (1885), commented explicitly and at length
on the feminism in the novel:

All the gentle seduction of talent of Miss Jewett seems to be concentrated
on one goal: to obtain the grace of the strong woman, the free woman, to
show what her strength and liberty cost her, how many female virtues
continue to flourish beneath male faculties acquired at the price of sacrifices which compel our respect, if not our sympathy.

Bentzon sees *A Country Doctor*, together with Jewett's earlier works,
as constituting a crusade in favor of the free woman.[35]

Literary criticism in the ensuing decades mainly ignored the
feminist argument that is at the heart of *A Country Doctor* and commented merely on its relevance as autobiography. Arthur Hobson
Quinn (1939), however, was a notable exception. After praising the
book as a fine narrative, he went on to complain that Nan's struggles between love and her profession are "less interesting."[36] If this
struggle was not interesting to Quinn, it has, however, become
increasingly interesting to some contemporary critics.

Ellen Morgan (1976) suggests that *A Country Doctor* is not feminist but rather represents a transition to feminism because the novel
accepts the limits of a patriarchal society. In refusing to accept
woman's traditional role, Nan is considered atypical of her sex.
Therefore, Morgan argues, the novel leaves unchallenged nineteenth-century assumptions about role expectations for most
women.[37] While it is true that Nan is described as atypical, the
many impassioned arguments in *A Country Doctor* are clearly intended to apply to many women and not only to Nan.

Josephine Donovan (1986), in contrast, sees that the central issue
in the novel grew out of the nineteenth-century women's rights

movement in that it confronts what she calls the "central theme of late nineteenth-century women's literature," namely whether to leave the world of mothers and venture into the patriarchal society that was just beginning to open up to women.[38]

Indeed, this is the issue upon which Sarah Orne Jewett constructed her tale of Nan's conflict. Like Elizabeth Cady Stanton, Charlotte Perkins Gilman, and other leading feminists of their generation, Nan understood that women needed meaningful work, and for some that meant moving into the male professions. Poised between the masculine and feminine realms, Nan chooses the role of her surrogate father, with the conviction that in so doing she will realize the promise of the fairy tale—to live happily ever after. The novel concludes with Nan thanking God for her future. The conclusion seems simplistic as a resolution to a political issue, but it works perfectly as fairy tale. *A Country Doctor* is ultimately a feminist myth.

NOTES

1. Francis Otto Matthiessen, *Sarah Orne Jewett* (Boston: Houghton Mifflin, 1929), p. 68.

2. Ibid., pp. 57–58.

3. As quoted in ibid., pp. 75–76.

4. Ibid., p. 73.

5. Sarah Orne Jewett, "Tom's Husband," *Atlantic Monthly* 49 (February 1882): 205–13.

6. See Joseph Donovan, "Nan Prince and the Golden Apples," *Colby Library Quarterly* 22 (1986); Malinda Snow, " 'That One Talent': The Vocation as Theme in Sarah Orne Jewett's *A Country Doctor*," *Colby Library Quarterly* 16 (1980); Richard Cary, *Sarah Orne Jewett* (New York: Twayne, 1962).

7. Matthiessen, *Sarah Orne Jewett*, p. 39.

8. As quoted in ibid., p. 41.

9. As quoted in ibid.

10. Sarah Orne Jewett, *A Country Doctor* (Boston: Houghton Mifflin, 1884), pp. 102–7. All further references to this work will be indicated parenthetically within the text. (Unavailable to the general reader for many years, *A Country Doctor* has just been reprinted by New American Library with an introduction which I wrote with Joy Gould Boyum.)

11. See Bruno Bettelheim, *The Uses of Enchantment: The Meaning and Importance of Fairy Tales* (New York: Vintage, 1977).

12. As quoted in Matthiessen, *Sarah Orne Jewett*, p. 108.

13. As quoted in ibid., p. 56.

14. As quoted in ibid., p. 84.

15. Per Seyersted, *Kate Chopin: A Critical Biography* (Baton Rouge: Louisiana State University Press, 1960), p. 52.

16. Willa Cather, Preface, *The Best Short Stories of Sarah Orne Jewett*, by Sarah Orne Jewett (Boston: Houghton Mifflin, 1925), p. xviii.

17. As quoted by Richard Cary, Foreword, *Appreciation of Sarah Orne Jewett: 29 Interpretive Essays* (Waterville, Me.: Colby College Press, 1973), pp. xi–xii.

18. Horace Scudder, "Miss Jewett," *Atlantic Monthly* 73 (January 1984): 130–33, rpt. in Cary, *Appreciation*, p. 17.

19. Edward Garnett, "Miss Sarah Orne Jewett's Tales," *Academy and Literature* 65 (July 11, 1903): 40–41, rpt. in Cary, *Appreciation*, p. 21.

20. Charles Miner Thompson, "The Art of Miss Jewett," *Atlantic Monthly* 94 (October 1904): 485–97, rpt. in Cary, *Appreciation*, p. 47.

21. Henry James, "Mr. and Mrs. Fields," *Cornhill Magazine* 39 (July 1915): 29–43, rpt. (with prior corrections of Henry James's New England geography) in *Atlantic Monthly* 116 (July 1915): 21–31.

22. Mary Ellman, "Phallic Criticism, *"Thinking About Women* (New York: Harcourt Brace Jovanovich, 1968), rpt. in *Women's Liberation and Literature*, ed. Elaine Showalter (New York: Harcourt Brace Jovanovich, 1971), pp. 213–22.

23. Fred Lewis Pattee, *The Development of the American Short Story* (New York: Harper, 1923), p. 263.

24. Vernon Parrington, *Main Currents in American Thought*, Vol. 3 (New York: Harcourt Brace, 1927–1930), p. 65.

25. Ludwig Lewisohn, *Expression in America* (New York: Harper, 1932), p. 289.

26. Granville Hicks, *The Great Tradition* (New York: Macmillan, 1933), p. 104.

27. Van Wyck Brooks, *New England: Indian Summer 1865–1915* (New York: E. P. Dutton, 1940), p. 353.

28. Carlos Baker, "Sarah Orne Jewett," in *Literary History of the United States*, Vol. 2, ed. Robert Spiller et al. (New York: Macmillan, 1948), pp. 845–47.

29. A. M. Buchan, *"Our Dear Sarah": An Essay on Sarah Orne Jewett*, New Series Language and Literature, no. 24 (St. Louis: Washington University Studies, 1953), p. 45.

30. Richard Cary, *Sarah Orne Jewett* (New York: Twayne, 1962), p. 64.

31. Barbara Solomon, Introduction, *Short Fiction of Sarah Orne Jewett and*

Mary Wilkins Freeman (New York: New American Library, 1979), pp. 1–2.

32. Josephine Donovan, *Sarah Orne Jewett* (New York: Frederick Ungar, 1980), p. 2.

33. Rev. of *A Country Doctor*, *Atlantic Monthly* 54 (September 1884): 419.

34. As quoted in Cary, *An Appreciation*, p. xii.

35. Th. Bentzon, "Le Roman de la Femme-Médecin, "*Revue des Deux Mondes* 47 (February 1, 1885): 598–632; English translation reprinted from *Colby Quarterly Review* (September 1967): 488–503, rpt. in Cary, *Appreciation*, pp. 8–9, 3.

36. Arthur Hobson Quinn, *American Fiction* (New York: Appleton-Century, 1939), p. 330.

37. Ellen Morgan, "The Atypical Woman: Nan Prince in the Literary Transition to Feminism," *Kate Chopin Newsletter* 2 (Fall 1976): 33–37.

38. Donovan, "Nan Prince and the Golden Apples," p. 2.

6

Matriarchy: Mary Wilkins Freeman, *Pembroke* (1894)

Mary Eleanor Wilkins (Freeman) was born in 1852 in Randolph, Massachusetts, a small New England town, which she re-created many times in her fiction. Randolph, like many other New England towns, was founded on middle-class Puritan ideals which stressed hard work, thrift, and Calvinist asceticism. Life was a struggle and money always scarce among the farmers and tradesmen and their families. This led to unstable social arrangements because the men frequently had to leave Randolph to get better jobs, and the women were forced to get husbands from other towns or remain single. Marriage was often a compromise based on economic necessity, a subject which is explored frequently in Freeman's fiction and especially in *Pembroke*.

Freeman's mother, Eleanor Lothrop, and her father, Warren Wilkins, were staunch Congregationalists who typified the hardworking middle class of Randolph. According to her biographer, Edward Foster, the Wilkins and Lothrop men were not particularly successful as providers and were therefore ruled by their wives.

When Freeman was fifteen the family moved to Brattleboro, Vermont, where she went to the local high school. She then attended Mount Holyoke Female Seminary for a year. Although there is a report of at least one romance at this time, Freeman remained unmarried, and in need of a livelihood she began to write verse and children's stories. After her parents' deaths she returned to Randolph, where in the ensuing years she wrote her major stories, which are collected in *A Humble Romance* (1887) and *A New England Nun* (1891), in addition to a number of novels, among which *Pembroke* (1894) is generally considered her masterpiece.

She did not marry until 1902, when at the age of forty-nine she chose Dr. Charles M. Freeman, a bachelor. Although the early years of the marriage are described by Freeman's biographers as happy, the relationship was increasingly troubled by Dr. Freeman's alcoholism and confinements in a mental hospital. In 1923, shortly before his death, Mary Wilkins Freeman obtained a legal separation from her husband.

When she died in 1930 she had published thirty-eight books, including fifteen novels and a number of collections of short stories. These books earned her a reputation as a realistic writer of distinction.

In Freeman's life as in her work, there seems always to be an uneasy tension between the feminine and feminist. While there is no record of her participation in the feminist cause of her time, there is considerable evidence of a desire to revolt and strike out for independence. Freeman is known to have read Emerson and been deeply impressed by his words, "Whoso would be a man must be a non-conformist." According to her friend Mrs. C. E. Severance. she was "encouraged by the rising tide of feminists" and "knew that she was right in reading 'man or woman' for the single word of the text."[1]

Also of interest in documenting Freeman's revolutionary tendencies is a piece of an unfinished story with obvious parallels to Freeman's own life situation at the time:

I am a rebel and what is worse a rebel against the Overgovernment of all creation. . . . I even dare to think that, infinitesimal as I am . . . I, through my rebellion, have power. All negation has power. I, Jane Lennox, spinster, as they would have designated me a century ago, living quietly, and apparently harmlessly in the old Lenox homestead in Baywater, am a power. . . .

I often wonder if I might not have been very decent, very decent indeed, if I had laid hold on the life so many of my friends lead. If I had only had a real home of my own with a husband and children in it. That was my birthright, but I was deprived of it, with neither trade nor barter.

And another thing which was my birthright: the character of the usual woman. I am a· graft on the tree of human womanhood. . . . I am a hybrid. Sometimes I think I am a monster, and the worst of it is, I certainly take pleasure in it. . . .

I sometimes wonder what would have been the state of the world had it not been for the Tables of Stone. . . .

Here am I, a woman, rather delicately built, of rather delicate tastes, perfectly able to break those commandments, to convert into dust every one of those Divine laws. I shudder before my own power, yet I glory because of it.[2]

The passage is a series of free associations, which are interesting in a number of ways. There is the suggestion that being a spinster is in itself an act of rebellion. For some reason a husband and children are viewed as a passport to decency, and by implication the single life for a woman is indecent. Indeed, the writer calls herself a "monster," but there is no evidence that she has done anything monstrous other than remain single. She does not indicate that she has ever broken any of the commandments, but is thrilled with the knowledge that she has the ability to do so. Being single is evidently viewed as somehow contrary to the norm and, therefore, not only an act of revolt but an evil. There is an ambivalence here about marriage, which is apparent also in Freeman's fiction. If marriage provides life's structure, it also impinges on freedom.

Despite the revolutionary message that permeates the fiction, there is in Freeman a decidedly feminine strain. In her life and work she remained keenly aware of the female role: to be pretty, to attract men, to marry, and to live in a domestic world surrounded by other women. Foster describes Freeman at thirty-two as "still pretty in a fragile, exquisite way. She knew that her blue eyes and red-gold hair were lovely, and she was fiercely determined to remain attractive." At this time in her life she wrote, "A man may write something that will live for the sake of something ignoble, and a woman may write something for money with which to buy a French hat."[3]

In describing Freeman's girlhood Foster suggests that she saw herself as a kind of Cinderella, expecting a princely person to claim her hand. By the time she wrote her fiction, these girlish dreams had been modified so that girls did not expect to be transformed by gallant heroes, but, nonetheless, the dreams of Freeman's heroines often focus on captivating the right man. If there is a contradiction between their feminism and femininity, it reflects the same contradiction in Freeman's own life.

Like other women writers, Freeman creates a woman-centered world. As Perry Westbrook has observed, "nine-tenths of the action takes place in the kitchen, the other tenth in the best parlor."[4] And the imagery is that of everyday farm life familiar to women.

If Freeman shared a style and method with other women writers, she herself was not aware of it. She insisted that every writer must found her own school and maintained that she was not influenced by any writers. Specifically she insisted that she had never read Jewett or Jane Austen and denied affinities that others found.

Despite her protests about literary influences, however, there was at least one writer Freeman greatly admired and who seems to have had some influence on her work, namely Emily Brontë. Freeman admired Brontë's ability to comprehend "primitive brutalities and passions" and praised *Wuthering Heights* as "an unflinching masterpiece," admirable in that there was no evidence "of feminine nerves in the mind or hand."[5] The statement is revealing in that it indicates what Freeman herself endeavored to create, namely the brutalities and passions of life, but it is also implicitly self-deprecating. The reference to feminine nerves suggests again Freeman's discomfort with her own femininity.

Noting the paucity of literature by and about women, especially before the eighteenth century, Virginia Woolf lamented that she had no way of knowing what they did from eight in the morning till eight at night.[6] Certainly the reader of American history has a similar problem. Except for a few words about suffrage, there is little in the texts to indicate that women were even there. If we wish to know what women did from eight in the morning till eight at night in nineteenth-century America, we must turn to literature and especially to fiction by women. Mary Wilkins Freeman's work in general and *Pembroke* in particular provide exactly the kind of insights for which Woolf searched in vain.

PEMBROKE

Pembroke bears the unmistakable stamp of the short story writer. It has a central plot flanked by several subplots, each of which could easily be a separate short story. The link among the stories is provided by the setting, which is a small New England town resembling Freeman's own hometown, Randolph, Massachusetts.

The novel depicts two generations of townspeople, most of whom are related. The perspective is always female, women providing the focus and men serving as satellites to matriarchal women, who are in charge of their own destinies and those of their families.

At least two of the central characters who people Pembroke are based on Freeman's family. The story of Barnabas and Charlotte, which forms the central plot of the novel, was based on the true story of Freeman's uncle, Barnabas. Freeman's maternal grandfather, Barnabas Lothrop, built a house for his son, Barnabas Junior, who was engaged to Mary Thayer. The wedding was planned, and all was in readiness when Barney became involved in an argument on politics with Mary Thayer's father. Mr. Thayer drove Barnabas from the house, and the marriage plans were terminated. Although Barney continued to love Mary, reconciliation never took place.

Freeman used this material from her family history to develop a larger purpose. In the introduction to the novel she explains that purpose as follows:

Pembroke was originally intended as a study of the human will in several New England characters, in different phases of disease and abnormal development, and to prove especially in the most marked case, the truth of a theory that its cure depended entirely upon the capacity of the individual for a love which could arise above all considerations of self, as Barnabas Thayer's love for Charlotte Barnard finally did. . . . Barnabas to me was as much the victim of disease as a man with curvature of the spine; he was incapable of straightening himself to his former stature until he had laid hands upon a more purely unselfish love than he had ever known, through his anxiety for Charlotte, and so raised himself to his own level.[7]

Although the twisted characters in the book are both male and female, the cure, if there is one, is always love, the special gift of women. Thus it is the women in the novel who hold the key to human redemption. They fail when they emulate men, however, and do not give the love that is essential to human life.

Pembroke does not address the Woman Question directly, but it is relevant here as it describes the roles of women and men in

American society from a woman's perspective. Freeman guides us
through a woman-centered world, showing us how women maintain dignity and independence in ways never imagined by those
who wrote in the leading journals of the day about what they presumed to be the roles God had given men and women. Freeman is
not polemical, but she has strong feelings about women and their
right to govern their own lives. Moreover, Freeman creates strong
women characters who belie the notion of the True Woman, which
was still being propounded by some.

The character in the novel who personifies ideal womanhood is
Charlotte Barnard. As the novel opens, Charlotte is about to be
wed to Barnabas Thayer. But a quarrel ensues between Charlotte's
father, Cephas, and Barney, which estranges the lovers for ten years.
Charlotte proves to be as good as she is beautiful. She is proud but
also loving, and it is her love which finally cures the deformity that
grows in Barney as he allows his life to be consumed by anger.
Though jilted by Barney, Charlotte is steadfast, refusing even the
proposal of the most eligible man in Pembroke. Finally, ten years
after the fateful evening when Barney was driven from Charlotte's
house, he becomes seriously ill. In his sickness he thinks of Charlotte and longs for "the eternal and protecting element in her love"
(p. 316), and Charlotte defies convention to nurse Barney. Barney
is described as a "rigidly twisted, groaning heap under a mass of
bedclothing" (p. 321). Nonetheless, when he finally understands
Charlotte's self-sacrifice, he walks to her house. Able at last to return the love he has received, he can stand tall again. Thus he finds
redemption through the love of a strong and good woman.

In contrast to Charlotte is Barney's mother, Deborah. Named
for the Old Testament Deborah, who is a judge, a prophetess, and
a warrior, Deborah Thayer is described as standing with "a pose
that might have answered for a statue of Judgment" (p. 56). And
while she is not literally a warrior like her Biblical namesake, "there
was that tone of command in her voice which only a woman can
accomplish. It was full of that maternal supremacy which awakens
the first instinct of obedience in man, and has more weight than
the voice of a general in battle" (p. 57). Deborah believes in original
sin and lives by a rigid moral code that represents the worst of
Calvinist narrow-mindedness and leaves little room for love. Thus,
she is sometimes admirable, but more often dangerous.

When Barney jilts Charlotte, Deborah is angry with her son for his failure to do his duty and act justly. But more often the puritanical tyranny of Deborah becomes a kind of moral numbness that interferes with real feeling. Deborah is unyielding, meeting life's problems by a maniacal devotion to daily duties. Thus when Deborah's first child dies she cleans all the windows in the house, and when Barnabas reneges on his marriage she makes sweet cake. When told of her younger son's heart disease, she simply refuses to recognize it. Deborah's energetic focus on work is seen as a life-sickening disease. When the family finally goes to bed, Deborah feels peace and security because she no longer has to confront the wills of others, and she concentrates all her energies upon her work. But in the end Deborah's puritanical self-righteousness causes her to whip her sickly son, Ephraim, for a minor infraction. He dies and she is blamed. Later she learns that his death was attributable to overexertion the previous evening, not to her whipping; but her grief is so great that it leads to her death. Her failure was clearly an inability to give love when it was needed.

Paralleling the love story of Barnabas and Charlotte is the love story of Charlotte's Aunt Sylvia and her beau of eighteen years, Richard Alger. Richard came to see Sylvia every Sunday night for eighteen years, and Sylvia's love for Richard sustained her through all those years. On the night that Cephas quarreled with Barney, Sarah Barnard, Sylvia's sister, detained her so that when Richard came to her door she could not be there. Richard assumes that she did not want to see him to accept the marriage proposal which he had hinted would be forthcoming that very evening. Freeman portrays this overly long courtship as both sad and absurd. The sexual reserve of the aging lovers is presented as unnecessary deprivation:

If her old admirer had, indeed, attempted to sit by her side upon that haircloth sofa and hold her hand, she would have arisen as if propelled by stiff springs of modest virtue. She did not fairly know that she was not made love to after the most honorable and orthodox fashion without a word of endearment or a caress; for she had been to regard love, as one of the most secret of the laws of nature, to be concealed, with shamefaced air, even from herself; but she did know that Richard had never asked her to marry him, and for that she was impatient without any self-reserve. (P. 26)

Grieved and distracted by her loss of Richard Alger, Sylvia one night mistakes Barnabas for Richard. In an effort to help the distracted Sylvia, Barney helps her into her house, but the situation is merely compounded as Sylvia persists in thinking that Barney is Richard. She asks him to put his arm around her, sobs on his shoulder, and confesses her misery. Barney realizes his deformity, which is his failure to realize love, a failure that inevitably destroys life. Happiness is finally achieved when Richard Alger rescues Sylvia as she is being moved unceremoniously to the poorhouse and finally marries her. The theme that love alone regenerates is thus underscored.

For her time Freeman shows a surprising candor about sex and sexuality. In treating the younger generation she frequently portrays an undercurrent of sexual attraction which the young people themselves do not fully comprehend. Scenes of cherry picking in Silas Berry's orchard provide the occasion for Freeman's depiction of youthful sexuality. In their innocence the young men and women do not recognize that the cherry picking becomes "a little bacchanalian rout in a New England field on a summer afternoon" (p. 138).

Although the young women in this rural New England village think almost constantly of marriage, practical considerations of money, family, or position are never at issue among this respectable Puritan stock. Instead they are driven by unacknowledged sexual passion, especially as depicted in the lives of Rose Berry and Rebecca Thayer.

The description of Rose conveys an overt sexuality rare in nineteenth-century American literature:

Rose's face between the green sides of bonnet had in it all the quickened bloom of youth in spring; her eyes had all the blue surprise of violets; she panted softly between red swelling lips as she walked; pulses beat in her crimson cheeks. Her slender figure yielded to the wind as to a lover. (P. 79)

Rose makes repeated advances to Barney only to be rejected because he is faithful to Charlotte. The explanation for Rose's infatuation is an unexpected revelation of girlish lust. Rose is described as a pagan who worships love itself. She is not punished for her sensuality as are so many heroines of nineteenth-century literature, but in the end she marries the boyish Tommy Ray and compromises with reality and respectability.

The story of Rebecca is more complicated. Like Charlotte, Rebecca affords maternal nurturing to her lover. Disgraced before his friends because of his father's stinginess in charging the young people for the privilege of berry picking in his orchard, William feels unworthy of Rebecca. But Rebecca wins his love by caring for him in his hurt. While Rebecca's sexuality is less overt than that of Rose, it is obvious to her puritanical mother, Deborah, who is unmoved by her daughter's desire for happiness. Deborah notes Rebecca's strange radiance only to oppose a marriage between William and Rebecca because of Barney's refusal to marry Charlotte, William's cousin. As Rebecca aptly observes, this hardly seems sufficient reason to oppose the match, but Deborah is steadfast.

Unwilling to oppose her parents, Rebecca refuses to marry William but continues to see him secretly. In due course she becomes pregnant and is ordered from the house by her unforgiving mother. Though Freeman recognizes sexuality as a vital part of female behavior, she cannot condone premarital sex. Rebecca has gone further than Rose, and she is punished accordingly.

Deborah immediately sends Barney to get William Berry so that he can marry Rebecca. William is willing to fulfill his obligations, but neither the bride nor groom evinces much happiness. On the wedding day Rebecca is reduced to a "muffled, hesitating figure" (p. 210), while William, waiting in the home of the village whore for his bride, must bear the full burden of his sin. When Rebecca's baby is finally born, it dies. The death seems retribution for the sin. In the end the Puritan code is upheld.

In the matriarchal society of Pembroke, men are often described as little boys to be nurtured or foolish children to be reprimanded. Hannah Berry sums up an attitude that prevails throughout most of the book when in discussing the quarrel between Barney Thayer and Cephas Barnard, she says:

It's just like two little boys—one wants to play marbles 'cause the other wants to play puss-in-the-corner, an' that's all the reason either of em's got for standin' out. Men ain't got too much sense anyhow when you come right down to it. They don't even get any too much grown up, the best of 'em. (P. 42)

This view of men implies a facile solution to the Woman Question. Obviously women have to do the work of the world because men, as here presented, are simply incompetent.

All of the male characters exhibit various degrees of ineptitude. Compared to wives and lovers, they always look somewhat inferior. While history shows that the work of men has generally been valued over the work of women, in *Pembroke* this is not the case. The work described in the novel is the household tasks of the women, and on one occasion when a man tries to do women's work, he fails dismally. Cephas Barnard decides that vegetarianism is an aid to spiritual health and therefore insists on preparing sorrel pies to take the place of his wife's meat pies. Sarah, Cephas's long-suffering wife, watches in despair as Cephas manages to prepare an inedible concoction. Deborah happens by and incredulously looks at Cephas, declaring, "You're making pies out of sorrel. A man makin' pies out of sorrel!" (p. 62). What is clearly implied is that a man is unfit to do women's work.

If Cephas Barnard is merely foolish, Silas Berry is worse still. Silas is a miser who manages to hurt and embarrass his children by his stinginess. As proprietor of a store, he argues childishly over a cent for sugar, and later permits his children, William and Rose, to have a cherry-picking party in his orchard only to demand payment from their guests after the fact.

Caleb Thayer, Deborah's husband, is another caricature of a man. Old and weak, he cowers before his wife's authoritarian posture. He attempts to comfort his sickly son, Ephraim, who trembles under his mother's thumb, but he is inevitably treated as just another recalcitrant child. Small gestures are telling. When she thought it was Caleb's bedtime, Deborah "shook Caleb with the force with which she might have shaken Ephraim. 'You'd better get up an' go to bed now, instead of sleepin' in your chair,' she said, imperatively; and Caleb obeyed, staggering, half-dazed, across the floor into the bedroom" (p. 153).

More attractive than their fathers, the younger generation of men is, nonetheless, equally impotent and dependent on the women who love them. When Barney refuses to marry Charlotte, he moves alone into his house, furnished with "a few simple bits of furniture," and sets up for "his miserable bachelor housekeeping." In contrast, "All the sweet domestic comfort which he had missed seemed suddenly to toss above his eyes like the one desired fruit of his whole life; its wonderful unknown flavor tantalized his soul" (p. 115). While the words apply specifically to Barney, they seem to represent the dreams of the other younger men as well. Their sole life interest appears to be in securing domestic comfort with the women of their choice. Indeed they represent the absolute polar opposite of the hero of classic American literature, the lonely adventurer in the wilderness.

Freeman's fictitious world thus avoids the realities of patriarchal society. If men governed a society from which women were still largely excluded, in *Pembroke* reality is turned on its heels. The world is a matriarchy with domesticity at its core, and men dream of happy homes rather than of great adventure. Instead of answering the Woman Question, Freeman denies it. Women's rights are unquestioned in the tiny world of Pembroke, and men are allowed to operate in that world mainly under the direction of women.

CRITICISM

Although little known in our own time, Mary Wilkins Freeman enjoyed a sound critical reputation among her contemporaries and over the years earned the praise of some of America's leading literary critics. Noted more for her short stories than her novels, she has earned praise especially for specific stories and for her overall vision. As for *Pembroke*, a number of critics have questioned whether it is a novel at all, its episodic structure and many subplots suggesting, as mentioned earlier, several short stories loosely strung together. Nonetheless, *Pembroke* has received limited but enthusiastic recognition over the years.

Conan Doyle called *Pembroke* the best novel written in America since *The Scarlet Letter*.[8] And Edwin Arlington Robinson (1894) commented that some of the scenes in the novel are "magnificent in their treatment."[9] Perry Westbrook (1967) praised *Pembroke* as being as true to New England life as the works of Hawthorne and Emily Dickinson. Despite this enthusiastic response by a few, however, the critical establishment has bypassed *Pembroke* in favor of Freeman's stories.

Since *Pembroke* is typical of Freeman's tales of New England, the critical commentary which looks beyond *Pembroke* at Freeman's entire work is particularly germane here. Early praise came from William Dean Howells (1887), who praised the stories as "peculiarly American" and representative of "the best modern work everywhere in their directness and simplicity."[10] Even more laudatory than her American contemporaries were Freeman's British readers. In 1890 the New York *Critic* commented, "There is something like a craze in England over Mary E. Wilkins." And in 1891 after the publication of *A New England Nun*, Freeman's first collected volume of short stories, the *London Spectator* declared, "The stories are among the most remarkable feats of what we may call literary impressionism in our language, so powerfully do they stamp on the reader's mind the image of the classes of individuals they portray without spending on the picture a single, redundant word, a single superfluous word."[11] In 1891 Freeman's English publisher wrote to her of the admiration of Henry James, who he said had "the greatest opinion" of her stories.[12] Freeman was also noted in France, where Th. Bentzon stated in 1896, "Miss Wilkins enjoys a spontaneity of expression, a strong sense of realism, a poetic talent, and a painter's skill that enables her to sketch a landscape in one or two strokes."[13]

In America Charles M. Thomson wrote the first extended analysis of Freeman's work in the *Atlantic Monthly* in 1899. He praised the literary merit of her stories and noted her feminine perspective. He also observed that although she was considered a realist, the mysticism and allegory that inhered in her work linked her to Hawthorne.[14] And Arthur Machen (1902) classified Freeman's work as "real literature" because he saw in it an understanding of human emotion, a kind of poetry.[15]

Amid the praise, however, there was at least one dissenting view, that of Grant Martin Overton (1918), who complained that Howells had unduly inflated the worth of Freeman's work, claiming a "literary value," which Overton denied. It was Overton's opinion that the stories were "slight, pleasing, sometimes entertaining, occasionally revelatory of human nature, but never for a moment revealing anything unexpected."[16]

More serious attention to the subtleties of Freeman's work was offered by Fred Lewis Pattee (1922). It was he who first noted Freeman's admiration for Emily Brontë and understood that though they led the sheltered lives appropriate to young girls in secluded villages, each had a rare capacity to understand human suffering of a depth and variety that she herself could not have experienced directly. He also saw her affinity with Hawthorne in that both were fostered by New England Puritanism and both were romancers and poets. Moreover he felt that she surpassed him in her "command of gripping situation" and "compelling characterization."[17]

Brief mention was made of Freeman by Blanche Colton Williams (1926), who noted merely that Freeman would be remembered for the stories of village and country life of a passing era.[18]

After her death in 1930, Freeman continued to attract the attention of literary critics. F. O. Matthiessen called Freeman "unsurpassed . . . among all American writers in her ability to give the breathless intensity of a moment." He placed her in a group of women writers who chronicled what he called "the New England ebb-tide," a society which was fading into oblivion by the end of the century.[19]

In the same year, John Macy also observed a female tradition in American literature in which Mary Wilkins Freeman occupied a prominent place. He saw Freeman and Jewett as the leading New England writers and noted that they had no successors. He praised Freeman as a "genius" and an "artist" who let the life about her speak for itself.[20] Van Wyck Brooks (1940) underscored what earlier critics had observed when he commended Freeman for her artistry and the "depth of feeling that informed her art."[21]

Soon after Brooks's glowing comments, interest in Mary Wilkins Freeman seems to have waned. She was barely mentioned or omitted entirely in critical commentaries on American literature; anthologies used in college classrooms rarely included her work. In 1966 Sylvia Townsend Warner wrote a piece for the *New Yorker* in which she apologetically defended her admiration for a little-known American writer named Mary Wilkins Freeman. She recounts how she told her dinner partner of her interest in Freeman only to be answered with an "Indeed" and a comment that "she wasn't thought much of now." Undaunted, Warner continued to admire Freeman, who she felt wrote with "a riveting authenticity." Like critics before her, Warner noted Freeman's difficulty in coming to grips with male characters, but this did not deter her from finding in Freeman a special quality "already found in nature and in certain teapots— something akin to the precision with which the green ruff fits the white strawberry blossom, or the airy spacing of a Worcester sprig."[22] Warner clearly understood the female perspective of Freeman's work.

Only a year after Warner's discovery of Freeman, Perry Westbrook published a valuable critical biography in which he called
Freeman "our most truthful recorder in fiction of New England
village life."[23]

Renewed interest in work by women writers in recent years has
led to inclusion of some of Freeman's work in new anthologies.
Many of her best stories were also collected in 1979 in the Signet
Classic *Short Fiction of Sarah Orne Jewett and Mary Wilkins Freeman*.
In her detailed introduction Barbara Solomon states that the stories
are limited by the boundaries of the small New England town the
characters inhabit, but that the tales reveal "the richness of the
inner landscape."[24]

We can only speculate on why the work of Mary Wilkins Freeman was neglected for such a long period. Once more the words
of Virginia Woolf may provide the key. Commenting on the difficulties faced by a woman writer who must face a male critical establishment, Woolf wrote that male and female values differ, and
it is the male values which prevail. Thus football is deemed "important," while fashion and buying clothes are called "trivial." Similarly a book dealing with war is considered valuable, while one
that deals with "the feelings of women in a drawing room" is dismissed as insignificant.[25] If Woolf is correct, and I think she is,
then it is not surprising that Mary Wilkins Freeman, who saw the
life of New England through the eyes of women, has been bypassed for several generations, and that only now, with the re-
emergence of feminism, is she beginning to be noted once again for
her contribution to American literature.

NOTES

1. See Edward Foster, *Mary E. Wilkins Freeman* (New York: Hendricks
House, 1956), p. 20.

2. As quoted in ibid., p. 34.

3. As quoted in ibid., p. 33.

4. Perry Westbrook, *Mary Wilkins Freeman* (New York: Twayne, 1967),
pp. 50–51.

5. "Emily Brontë and Wuthering Heights," in *The Book Lover's Reading
Club Hand-Book . . . The World's Great Woman Novelists* (Philadelphia, 1901),
pp. 88–89, as quoted in Foster, *Mary E. Wilkins Freeman*, p. 135.

6. Virginia Woolf, *A Room of One's Own* (New York: Harcourt, Brace, 1929), p. 48.

7. Mary E. Wilkins Freeman, *Pembroke* (1894, rpt. New York: Harper, 1899), p. iii. All further references to this work will be indicated parenthetically within the text.

8. See Westbrook, *Mary Wilkins Freeman*, p. 103.

9. Letter to Harry DeForest Smith, October 28, 1894, as quoted in Westbrook, *Mary Wilkins Freeman*, p. 103.

10. William Dean Howells, "Editor's Study," *Harper's New Monthly* 74 (1887): 640.

11. As quoted in Fred Lewis Pattee, "On the Terminal Moraine of New England Puritanism," in *Sidelights on American Literature* (New York: Century, 1922), pp. 186–87.

12. See Foster, *Mary E. Wilkins Freeman*, p. 89.

13. Th. Bentzon, "Un Romancier de la Nouvelle-Angleterre," *Revue des Deux Mondes* 136 (1896): 544–569, as quoted in Westbrook, *Mary Wilkins Freeman*, p. 173.

14. Charles M. Thomson, "Miss Wilkins: An Idealist in Masquerade," *Atlantic Monthly* 83 (1899): 669.

15. Arthur Machen, *Hieroglyphics* (1902, rpt. London: Unicorn, 1960), pp. 173–75.

16. Grant Martin Overton, *The Women Who Make Our Novels* (New York: Moffat, Yard, 1918), pp. 198–99.

17. Pattee, "Terminal Moraine," p. 209.

18. Blanche Colton Williams, *Our Short Story Writers* (New York: Dodd, Mead, 1926), p. 180.

19. Francis Otto Matthiessen, "New England Short Stories," in *American Writers on American Literature*, ed. John Macy (New York: Horace Liveright, 1931), pp. 399–400.

20. John Macy, "The Passing of the Yankee," *Bookman* 73 (1931): 617.

21. Van Wyck Brooks, *New England Indian Summer 1865–1915* (New York: E. P. Dutton, 1940), p. 465.

22. Sylvia Townsend Warner, "Item, One Empty House," *New Yorker*, March 26, 1966, pp. 131–34.

23. Westbrook, *Mary Wilkins Freeman*, p. 15.

24. Barbara Solomon, *Short Fiction of Sarah Orne Jewett and Mary Wilkins Freeman* (New York: New American Library, 1979), p. 38.

25. Woolf, *A Room of One's Own*, pp. 76–77.

7

Rebellion and Death: Kate Chopin, *The Awakening* (1899)

Born in St. Louis in 1851, Kate Chopin was the daughter of an Irish immigrant father and an American mother of French extraction. In 1870 Kate O'Flaherty married Oscar Chopin, a French-Creole. There is little in her early life that presages Chopin's interest in the Woman Question, but one detail merits attention. On her honeymoon in Europe Chopin met one of the Claflin sisters. In her diary Chopin wrote, "She entreated me not to fall into the useless degrading life of most married ladies—but to elevate my mind and turn my attention to politics, commerce, questions of state, etc., etc. I assured her I would do so."[1]

Nonetheless, after her marriage Chopin led a conventional life. She moved with Oscar to Louisiana, where she lived among the French-Creoles she depicts in her work. In due course she had six children and with her young family spent summers at Grand Isle, a resort in the Gulf of Mexico frequented by the Creoles of Vieux Carré.

The marriage between Oscar and Kate Chopin was, according to Chopin's first biographer, Daniel Rankin, a happy one. Her life during her marriage was largely devoted to the duties of mother and society woman, and she appeared content with her role. But the marriage ended precipitately in 1883 with the death of Oscar.

Alone and in need of money, she was urged by Dr. Frederick Kolbenheyer, her obstetrician and a close friend, to attempt to augment her income through writing. Her mentors were writers she avidly read. Her debt to DeMaupassant and Flaubert has been widely acknowledged, but little has been written about her admiration for American women writers of her generation. Commenting on a neighbor's literary efforts, she wrote:

If she were younger I would tell her to study critically some of the best of our short stories. I know of no one better than Miss Jewett to study for the technique and nicety of construction. I don't mention Mary E. Wilkins (Freeman) for she is a great genius, and genius is not to be studied.[2]

Elsewhere Chopin declared Freeman's novel *Pembroke* to be "the most powerful piece of fiction of its kind that has ever come from the American press."[3]

Chopin's literary output was small, consisting of only one novel in addition to *The Awakening* and a number of short stories. *The Awakening* (1899) marked the end of Chopin's brief literary career because she was so discouraged by its negative reception. When Chopin died in 1904 she was practically forgotten, and she continued in near oblivion for half a century.

Kate Chopin was never politically involved with the women's rights movement, but her works reveal that she was immersed in the issues of her time. Like so many feminist activists of the nineteenth century, Chopin frequently examined the institution of marriage. And it is marriage that is a central issue in *The Awakening*. On the surface there is little similarity between the happy marriage of Kate Chopin and the disintegrating marriage of her protagonist, Edna Pontellier. But it seems that in writing about Edna, Chopin was often thinking about herself. Edna, like Kate Chopin, was an outsider among French-Creoles. She was born in Mississippi and raised in Kentucky, and like her creator, she was the daughter of "an American woman with a small infusion of French."[4] Neither Kate Chopin nor Edna Pontellier was really part of the social milieu of Grand Isle, where both Chopin and Edna spent summers with their children.

The correspondence of certain biographical details between Kate Chopin and Edna Pontellier is not in itself remarkable. What is perhaps more compelling is that Kate Chopin's own feelings are frequently projected onto her heroine. For example, in describing Edna's exultation at hearing certain kinds of music, Chopin was apparently describing her own feelings. After listening to an admired violinist, Chopin confided the following to her diary:

> To describe the effect his music had upon me would be impossible. It seemed the very perfection of the art, and while listening to him, I for the first time longed to be blind that I might drink it all in undisturbed and undistracted by surrounding objects.[5]

This same feeling is described in *The Awakening* when Edna listens to Mlle. Reisz play the piano:

> She saw no pictures of solitude, of hope, of longing, or of despair. But the very passions themselves were aroused within her soul, swaying it, lashing it, as the waves daily beat upon her splendid body. She trembled, she was choking, and the tears blinded her. (P. 27)

The piece which evokes this emotion was written by Frédéric Chopin, and Edna entitled it "Solitude." Within Kate Chopin there seems to have been a deep longing for solitude that could not be rationally explained, and this longing was re-created within Edna.

Similar unexplained emotions are noted by Daniel Rankin, who says that Edna's moods were those of the author. Chopin writes in the novel: "There were days she was very happy without knowing why. She was happy to be alone and breathing. . . . There were days when she was unhappy, she did not know why,—when life appeared to her like a grotesque pandemonium" (p. 58). Rankin suggests that Chopin might have been describing herself.

It appears that Chopin's own discontent and longing for solitude were expressed only in the privacy of her diary and in her fiction. One can only speculate whether her fiction also represents her own experience of the constraints of nineteenth-century marriage, not only in *The Awakening* but in her only other novel, *At Fault*, and in several of her short stories, all of which explore a woman's discontent in marriage. Like her feminist sisters who were active in the women's rights movement, she often subjects the institution of marriage to meticulous scrutiny.

THE AWAKENING

A short novel, only a little over 100 pages, *The Awakening* focuses narrowly on its protagonist. Edna Pontellier is a pretty young woman married to a comfortable businessman, who provides well for her and expects that in exchange she will perform her role as wife, mother, and society matron. Edna and Léonce, her husband, do not appear to value each other's company, and, therefore, they lead lives quite independent of one another. On weekdays during the summer vacation Léonce goes to the city to work while his wife and their two sons remain at Grand Isle. On weekends he appears at Grand Isle but seems to spend most of his time with other New Orleans club men. Chopin describes all this with detachment; certainly the pattern was not unusual.

We are told that despite her marriage to a Creole, Edna does not feel at home in the society of Creoles. Therefore, she misunderstands the attentions of Robert Lebrun, a young man who attaches himself to her, as he had attached himself to other women at the resort in previous years. When Robert realizes that they may be falling in love, he leaves abruptly for Mexico. Once he is gone Edna recognizes more than ever the intensity of her infatuation.

At the same time she realizes the hollowness of her marriage and step by step begins to emancipate herself from a lifestyle which demanded that she satisfy Mr. Pontellier's expectations. The result is growing contention between the two:

Mr. Pontellier had been a rather courteous husband so long as he met a certain tacit submissiveness in his wife. But her new and unexpected line of conduct completely bewildered him. It shocked him. Then her absolute disregard for her duties as a wife angered him. When Mr. Pontellier became rude, Edna grew insolent. She had resolved never to take another step backward. (P. 57)

Finally Edna moves out of the mansion she had shared with her husband and into her own small house.

One afternoon she meets a fashionable roué, Alcée Arobin, and finds herself passionately attracted though not in love. Soon thereafter Robert returns from Mexico, but he does not visit her. They meet by chance and then later that day declare their love. But Robert is unwilling to compromise another man's wife and leaves Edna. She returns to Grand Isle alone and commits suicide by walking quietly into the ocean. Freedom is achieved only through total renunciation.

As the novel unfolds, Edna gradually emerges from caged domesticity only to find that there is no way for her to realize her freedom in the world in which she lives. Chopin begins her narrative with an image of two caged birds—a mocking bird and a parrot that keeps repeating the phrase, "*Allez vous-en! Allez vous-en! Sapristi!*" (Go away! Go away! For God's sake!) The birds in their cages, we are told, can make all the noise they wish, but "Mr. Pontellier had the privilege of quitting their society when they ceased to be entertaining" (p. 9). In fact, that is precisely what he does. Shortly after we are introduced to Mr. Pontellier, Edna returns from swimming. Mr. Pontellier exchanges a few casual remarks with her, yawns, and decides to go to Klein's Hotel to play billiards. Although their children have a nurse, the expectation is that Edna will stay home to see that they are properly cared for. She has learned to accept this as unquestioningly as the parrot and the mocking bird accept their cages. Indeed, before Mr. Pontellier leaves, he gives his wife her rings, which he had held while she swam. In accepting them Edna symbolically gives tacit consent to the marital conventions.

A little while later Mr. Pontellier returns and announces that one of the children has a fever, and he chides his wife for neglecting them, thus making it clear that the responsibility for the children is assumed to belong totally to their mother. Nonetheless, Mr. Pontellier is far from the villain of the piece; rather he is described as a model nineteenth-century husband. When he is in the city he sends his wife gifts of bonbons, patés, and fruit, and "all declared that Mr. Pontellier was the best husband in the world" (p. 9).

The basis of the Pontellier marriage is largely economic. Mr. Pontellier regards his wife as "a valuable piece of personal property" (p. 4) and expects that she will fulfill her domestic role in return for material things. In describing the Pontellier mansion in New Orleans, the authorial voice tells us, "The cut glass, the silver, the heavy damask which daily appeared upon the table were the envy of many women whose husbands were less generous than Mr. Pontellier" (p. 50).

The situation in the Pontellier household recalls views on marriage articulated by Margaret Fuller and Charlotte Perkins Gilman, who perceived that a woman's financial dependence on a man resulted in her subordinate position.[6] Edna perceives the inevitable link between money and independence when she moves out of her home and into the small "pigeon house" that she buys with her own funds. Explaining her move from the Pontellier mansion, she states, "The house, the money that provides it, are not mine" (p. 79), and the authorial voice adds, "whatever came she had resolved never again to belong to another than herself" (pp. 79–80).

Although events in the novel are generally seen from Edna's perspective, it is made clear that the fault in the marriage is Edna's as well as Mr. Pontellier's. Mr. Pontellier regrets that Edna cares little for his conversation and his concerns. But Edna suffers more than her husband because he can always lose himself in the world of business. After a weekend with his family, he looks forward to returning to a lively week in Carondelet Street, but she has to remain in an alien world of mothers and children.

Edna finds herself among "mother-women," who "idolize their children, worship their husbands, and esteem it a holy privilege to efface themselves as individuals and grow wings as ministering angels" (p. 10). But Edna is not satisfied to efface herself, and the responsibility for her children is one for which she feels fate has not fitted her. Motherhood is the most problematic aspect of Edna's life. Many roles can be stripped away, but motherhood is not easily relinquished. She confides to Dr. Mandelet, "I want to be let alone. Nobody has any right—except children, perhaps—and even then, it seems to me or it did seem—" (p. 109). The vacillation demonstrated in this statement is not characteristic of Edna as she moves toward greater and greater self-assurance in her quest for independence. Unable to accept the nineteenth-century expectations of motherhood, she is also unable to reject her children except through death. She tells Mme. Ratignolle, "I would give my money, I would give my life for my children; but I wouldn't give myself" (p. 48).

Surrounded by families in a confined environment, what Edna longs for is space and solitude, which she can achieve only momentarily when she swims out into the ocean. She dreams of swimming where no woman has ever swum before, but she imagines a barrier which she would not be able to overcome.

Although Edna senses from the beginning that departing from the norm is dangerous, she is determined to liberate herself from the constrictions placed upon her. Her first act of defiance is small. After returning from a swim with Robert, she decides to sleep outside in a hammock despite Mr. Pontellier's request that she come inside. Edna remembers that in the past she had submitted to her husband's wishes, but now she is firm in her resistance. By refusing Mr. Pontellier's request, Edna renounces both submissiveness and domesticity. Her domain is no longer the house but the open air.

Shortly thereafter Edna, to her husband's dismay, refuses to be "at home" on Tuesday afternoons and thereby begins a systematic tearing down of the conventional routines that had become her life. When Mr. Pontellier complains about his dinner and Edna's failure to oversee the cook, she no longer cries at his rebuke, as she had done when he scolded her about neglecting the children. Instead, when she is alone she takes off her wedding ring, throws it on the carpet, stamps on it, and strives to crush it. The marriage is not, however, destroyed so easily. The ring does not dent, and Edna's maid returns it to her. Still, the scene marks an important contrast with the earlier scene where she had willingly slipped the rings on her finger after her swim.

As Edna slowly but pointedly extricates herself from her marriage bonds, she observes the happy domestic life of the Ratignolles. Her conclusion is that theirs "was not a condition of life which fitted her" (p. 56). It is thus made clear that although submissive domesticity might be suitable for some, it cannot be the only option open to women; Edna must clearly have something else, but what that is seems to elude her.

Having refused to continue the "tacit submissiveness" that Mr. Pontellier had come to expect in his wife, Edna decides to set up a studio to paint. Predictably Mr. Pontellier objects. He declares, "It seems to me the utmost folly for a woman at the head of a household, and the mother of children, to spend in an atelier days which would be better employed contriving for the comfort of her family" (p. 57). But Edna refuses to listen as she experiments with a new role.

The life roles open to Edna are represented in the novel by two women: the "mother-woman," Adele Ratignolle, and the artist,

Mademoiselle Reisz. After rejecting the role of "mother-woman," Edna flirts with the idea of becoming an artist only to reject that as well. While Edna likes to paint, she does not consider herself an artist. In fact, the artist role seems as uncongenial to her as that of "mother-woman." Though Mademoiselle Reisz is unquestionably talented—perhaps even a genius—she is "the most disagreeable and unpopular woman who ever lived in Bienville Street" (p. 59). In being "self-assertive," she exhibits a "disposition to trample upon the rights of others." In addition she is "homely" and "had no taste in dress" (p. 26). And finally her false hair and the artificial violets that are always pinned to the side of her head suggest that she is at war with nature. The portrait of Mademoiselle Reisz could hardly be less attractive. In her devotion to art, she seems to have become unsexed, and Edna, despite her appreciation for Mademoiselle's talents, cannot identify with this unwomanly woman. While Edna, like Mademoiselle Reisz, "dares and defies" in many areas of her life, she appears unwilling to abandon her womanliness as Mademoiselle Reisz had done.

In a world where Charlotte Perkins Gilman had suggested a woman was "to be female and nothing else,"[7] there was at least one permissible area of concern outside the family, namely religion. But for Edna religion is as problematic as marriage. Questioned by Madame Ratignolle about her attitude toward religion, Edna confesses, "during one period of my life religion took a firm hold upon me; after I was twelve and until—until—why, I suppose until now, though I never thought much about it—just driven along by habit" (p. 18). The statement suggests that at the advent of puberty Edna accepted the notion of piety as she had accepted other aspects of secular womanhood, and yet her actions indicate that her rejection of religion, as of other conventions, has been progressive. While she is not aware of her motives, her behavior has been consistent.

When she was a little girl she had run away from the Presbyterian service of her father's church, which filled her with a chilling spirit of gloom. Her marriage with Mr. Pontellier was in part a rebellion against her father's Presbyterianism. At one point she claims that her decision to marry Mr. Pontellier was determined less by love than by "the violent opposition of her father and her sister Margaret to her marriage with a Catholic" (p. 19). But it is not only

Presbyterianism which is uncongenial to Edna. When Robert takes her to a Catholic church she feels oppressed and drowsy and seeks the open air. Edna's rejection of piety is underscored in the novel by a recurring vignette of lovers followed by a young woman in black carrying a rosary and a prayer book. The image suggests a choice between piety and love. Obliged to choose, Edna denies piety.

Edna's rebellion is complete when in addition to rejecting domesticity, submissiveness, and piety, she also rejects the most important attribute of True Womanhood, namely purity. This is not to imply that these are rejected in any particular order. Rather she was "daily casting aside that fictitious self which we assume like a garment with which to appear before the world" (p. 57), until at the end she stands naked before the open sea. The point to be emphasized is that purity is only one part of the fictitious self that is cast away as Edna awakens. A good deal of literary criticism has emphasized Edna's sexual awakening. Indeed, Kenneth Eble went so far as to say that "the book is about sex,"[8] but this interpretation is not really supported by the text.

The men in Edna's life are minor characters. Robert disappears in the first third of the book when he realizes that Edna cares for him, only to reappear near the end to tell her that their relationship is impossible. There is, in fact, no declaration of love or even any hint of physical involvement between Edna and Robert until their final meeting, and even then what occurs is hardly a torrid love scene. Their love is never consummated because Edna must leave to attend Madame Ratignolle in childbirth. Far from being a burning lover, Robert is as conventional as Mr. Pontellier. He refuses to have an illicit affair and departs from Edna's life with a note: "I love you. Good-by—because I love you" (p. 111).

Edna's infatuation with Robert is almost as much illusion as her girlish infatuations for a calvary officer, a nameless young gentleman who courted a lady on a neighboring plantation, and a great tragedian, whom she never met. It was when Robert is away in Mexico that Edna's sexuality is first aroused. Bored and lonely, she takes up with Arobin, whom she does not love. Nonetheless, when he kisses her, we are told, "It was the first kiss of her life to which her nature had really responded. It was a flaming torch that had kindled desire" (p. 83). It is only in her brief affair with Arobin

that Edna loses sexual innocence. But Arobin is even more incon-
sequential than Robert. Edna comes to realize, "To-day it is Arobin; tomorrow it will be some one else" (p. 113).

The whole issue of Edna's having lovers is central to the novel
only insofar as it marks one more attempt to break the chain of
convention that holds Edna in a loveless marriage. The point is
made explicit when Edna rebukes Robert for dreaming that Mr.
Pontellier would set her free. She tells him: "You have been a very
foolish boy, wasting your time dreaming of impossible things when
you speak of Mr. Pontellier's setting me free! I am no longer one
of Mr. Pontellier's possessions to dispose of or not. I give myself
where I choose" (p. 107). To give oneself where one chooses is the
ultimate denial of the traditional female role. Robert himself is incidental. Edna comes to realize "that the day would come when he
[Robert], too, and the thought of him would melt out of her existence, leaving her alone" (p. 113).

Having stripped herself of her social roles, Edna in the end seems
to have no recourse but suicide. There is little agreement among
critics as to what Edna's suicide signifies. At one extreme is the
view of George Spangler, who insists that Chopin's conclusion is
not an integral part of the work, and that it merely provides "pa-
thos to please sentimental readers and justice to satisfy moralistic
ones."[9] At the other extreme is Judith Fryer's view that the main
patterns of the book come together in its final passage detailing
Edna's thoughts and feelings as she drowns herself.[10] An examination of the novel's conclusion suggests that Fryer is nearer the truth.
The long lyrical passage that concludes the novel is a collage of
Edna's life:

The voice of the sea is seductive, never ceasing, whispering, clamoring,
murmuring, inviting the soul to wander in abysses of solitude. . . . A
bird with a broken wing was beating the air above, reeling, fluttering,
circling disabled down, down to the water. . . . How strange and awful
it seemed to stand naked under the sky! how delicious! She felt like some
newborn creature, opening its eyes in a familiar world that it had never
known. . . . She did not look back now, but went on and on, thinking of
the blue-grass meadow that she had traversed when a little child, believing
that it had no beginning and no end. . . . She thought of Léonce and the
children. They were a part of her life. But they need not have thought
that they could possess her, body and soul. How Mademoiselle Reisz would

have laughed, perhaps sneered, if she knew! "And you call yourself an artist!" What pretensions, Madame! The artist must possess the courageous soul that dares and defies. "Good-by—because I love you." He did not know; he did not understand. Perhaps Doctor Mandelet would have understood if she had seen him—but it was too late; the shore was far behind her, and her strength was gone. . . . She looked into the distance, and the old terror flamed up for an instant, then sank again. Edna heard her father's voice and her sister Margaret's. She heard the barking of an old dog that was chained to the sycamore tree. The spurs of the cavalry officer clanged as he walked across the porch. There was the hum of bees, and the musky odor of pinks filled the air. (Pp. 113–14)

The images form a kaleidoscope of Edna's world—the sea, the bluegrass meadow of Edna's childhood, the children, Mr. Pontellier, Robert's note, Dr. Mandelet, her father's voice, and the sound of the cavalry officer's spurs. An examination of these images suggests the conflicting aspects of Edna's life, in which the desire for freedom and solitude were often circumscribed by a sense of social expectations and responsibility as well as a need for love and romance.

The sea and meadow are associated in Edna's mind with freedom and solitude. Early in the novel she had told her friend Madame Ratignolle of

a meadow that seemed as big as the ocean to the very little girl walking through the grass, which was higher than her waist. She threw out her arms as if swimming when she walked, beating the tall grass as one strikes out in the water. . . . I could see only the stretch of green before me, and I felt as if I must walk on forever, without coming to the end of it. I don't remember whether I was frightened or pleased. (Pp. 17–18)

There is in this description of the meadow the same ambivalence Edna felt about the ocean, which gave her an "impression of space and solitude" but also frightened her (p. 29).

Léonce, the children, and Mlle. Reisz represent in this final passage of the novel the responsibilities and life roles Edna rejected. She was unable to find satisfaction as wife, mother, or artist. And the dreams of romance suggested by the reference to the cavalry officer's spurs were after all nothing but dreams.

But what are we to make of the elliptical reference to Dr. Man-

delet and to Robert's failure to understand? Biographical information might be helpful in explaining what remains elusive in the
text. Dr. Mandelet appears to be a fictional re-creation of Dr. Frederick Kolbenheyer, Chopin's obstetrician and friend, who was
mentioned earlier as having been instrumental in her writing career. Dr. Kolbenheyer seems to have understood that a woman
needed work of her own to provide both money and satisfaction.
But in the novel the doctor is not given the opportunity to help.
Edna dies without seeking the assistance he promised if she would
come to see him.

Although we are never told what Dr. Mandelet might have
understood, some hints are provided earlier in the text. At one
point Mr. Pontellier had confided to Dr. Mandelet, "She's got some
sort of notion in her head about the eternal rights of women" (p. 65).
Dr. Mandelet demonstrates that he understands this notion far better than Mr. Pontellier when later on he explains to Edna: "The
trouble is . . . that youth is given up to illusions. It seems to be a
provision of Nature, a decoy to secure mothers for the race. And
Nature takes no account of moral consequences, of arbitrary conditions which we create, and which we feel obliged to maintain at
any cost" (pp. 109–10). These words are spoken immediately after
Edna has assisted with Madame Ratignolle's childbirth, which she
views as a "scene of torture" (p. 109). While the passage suggests
that biological determinism is a cause of women's oppression, the
novel is more concerned with the "arbitrary conditions which we
create."

What Edna wants is simply to be a human being. Early in the
novel we are told, "Mrs. Pontellier was beginning to realize her
position in the universe as a human being and to recognize her
relations as an individual to the world within and about her" (pp. 14–
15). But being a human being is precisely what is denied her. As
she strips away all the vestiges of her womanly role, she finds herself alone and disconnected from a world in which people are narrowly circumscribed in social roles.

Finally, there is in the novel's concluding passage the allusion to
the voice of Edna's father. He plays a very small role in the novel,
but whenever he is mentioned he appears to represent the worst of
patriarchal society. He was a colonel who "had coerced his own
wife into her grave" (p. 71). And when he visits Edna, he "kept

her busy serving him and ministering to his wants" (p. 69). When, however, Edna defies the patriarchy, she is either confined in a "pigeon house" or alone in an empty ocean. Her successive steps toward emancipation lead her not to happiness but to death.

CRITICISM

The Awakening has generated a good deal of contradictory criticism. Perhaps the difficulty in interpretation grows out of the ambiguity of the authorial stance. Is one to admire, condemn, or pity Edna? Chopin gives us no precise answers. Edna is sensitive and unhappy, but she is also often petulant, inconsiderate, and narcissistic.

On first publication in 1899 *The Awakening* was condemned as "gilded dirt," a new entry into "the overworked field of sex fiction," and a story about the "loathsome monster Passion."[11] Accordingly, the book was soon removed from library shelves. Even so astute a reader as Willa Cather found it "trite and sordid," despite stylistic merits that she and many other critics also noted.[12] Only one review, that of C. L. Deyo, pleased the author. Deyo was the only contemporary reviewer who understood that the book was not about sex. He wrote, "It is the life and not the mask that is the subject of the story." He alone perceived that Edna was more to be pitied than blamed: "She had no anchor and no harbor was in sight."[13] Chopin wrote of Deyo's review, "It seems so able and intelligent by contrast with some of the drivel I have run across."[14]

Kate Chopin and *The Awakening* were soon forgotten. American literary histories before 1950 either ignore the book entirely or dismiss it briefly. Arthur Hobson Quinn (1936) praises Chopin's stories but calls *The Awakening* "a work of morbid psychology."[15] Carlos Baker likewise praises Chopin's short stories but does not even mention *The Awakening*.[16]

By the 1950s critics began to notice the novel, but little attention was paid to its thematic content. Clarence Gohdes (1951) compared it to *Madame Bovary* and suggested that "it deserves a worthy place in the history of sterner realism in nineteenth-century America."[17] And Van Wyck Brooks called it "a small perfect work that mattered more than the whole life work of many a prolific writer."[18] In 1956 Kenneth Eble wrote the first extended discussion of *The*

Awakening in an article mentioned earlier, entitled "A Forgotten Novel: Kate Chopin's *The Awakening*" (1956). The article became the introduction when the novel was finally reissued in 1964. While Eble did not condemn the sexuality in the novel, as earlier critics had done, his emphasis on the novel's sexual aspects in some ways echoed the earliest reviews.

Renewed interest in women writers in the 1960s and 1970s led to both a rediscovery and a reassessment of *The Awakening*. Some critics saw it mainly in feminist terms as a work which sheds light on the position of women in nineteenth-century America. Suzanne Wolkenfield affirms a position taken here, namely that the portrayal of Adele Ratignolle and Mademoiselle Reisz is intended to suggest the roles open to women.[19] And Jules Chametzky adds that "the woman's question" posed in the book is "how to be free in one's self but still meaningfully connected to others."[20] Lawrence Thornton presents yet another view, which has also been presented here: "The New Woman . . . demands the prerogatives of men, but in making these demands she can only be destroyed by overreaching in a society that holds no place for her." He declares that she fails at freedom because "she cannot see beyond the romantic prison of imagination."[21]

When Edmund Wilson first commented on *The Awakening* in *Patriotic Gore* (1962), he seemed more puzzled than enlightened by the book:

It is a very odd book to have been written in America at the end of the nineteenth century. It is not even a "problem novel." No case for free love or women's rights or the injustice of marriage is argued. The heroine is simply a sensuous woman who follows her inclinations without thinking much about these issues or tormenting herself with her conscience.[22]

Seven years later, however, in the foreword to Per Seyersted's *The Complete Works of Kate Chopin* (1969), Wilson's apparent puzzlement gave way to an understanding that Chopin wrote from a feminist perspective, which many of her early readers found unacceptable:

She was attempting to put on record the real inner emotions of women in relation to their men and their children, and it was this that made the hair stand on end of those genteel readers of the nineties and that caused her

to be blackballed when proposed for membership in the St. Louis Fine
Arts Club. It was this that caused her to be reprobated by the so snob-
bishly moral reviewers of that era.[23]

Another group of critics has attempted to place *The Awakening* in
the context of European and American literature of its time, but
the differences seem at least as compelling as the similarities. Lewis
Leary says that Edna Pontellier is "worthy of a place beside other
fictional heroines who have tested emancipation and failed—Na-
thaniel Hawthorne's Hester Prynne, Gustave Flaubert's Emma
Bovary or Henry James's Isabel Archer."[24] There is no question
that Edna fails every bit as much as her fictional sisters, but Hawthorne, Flaubert, and James suggest in their novels a moral conflict
within their heroines which is absent from *The Awakening*. While
the male writers mentioned above do not necessarily approve the
society in which their protagonists live, there is an assumption that
unless one accepts the rules, suffering must be endured. Edna in
contrast is portrayed without moral compunction. She leaves the
world she found uncongenial without ever conceding that there was
a legitimate moral alternative in a society she did not help create.
  Had she been male, there might have been an alternative. The
male protagonist, particularly in American literature of the nineteenth century, found legitimate means to leave the confines of an
inhibiting society. Ishmael could go to sea, Huck Finn could "light
out for the Territory," and Natty Bumpo could explore the fron-
tier. But for women there seemed no escape except in death.
  Attempts to place *The Awakening* in America's romantic tradition
also seem forced because the novel is not sufficiently analogous to
any other novel. For example, Donald Ringe says, "*The Awakening*
is a powerful romantic novel," and suggests that Chopin presents
Edna "in terms suggesting Melville—as a solitary defiant soul who
stands against the limitations that both nature and society place
upon her."[25] But Melville's protagonists are able to live at sea or
on tropical islands, while Edna dies. Lewis Leary finds that "the
whole of *The Awakening* is pervaded with the spirit of Whitman's
'Song of Myself' ";[26] however, Whitman's song is joyous in contrast to Chopin's, which ultimately becomes a dirge.
  George Arms and Kenneth Eble look for meaning in the brief
episode where Edna falls asleep reading Emerson. Eble suggests

that Edna's reading of Emerson is a reaction against her father's
Presbyterianism, and Arms adds that "to grow sleepy over a Tran-
scendental individualist also hints that Edna's individualism lacks
philosophical grounding."[27] Perhaps, but it is also possible that she
grows sleepy because she can find nothing in Emerson's view of
individualism which relates to a woman of her time. While Mary
Wilkins Freeman believed that Emerson meant human beings when
he spoke of men, her belief was little more than wishful thinking.
Writing about women, Emerson suggested that far from being in-
diviudals acting in accord with nature, women were totally dependent and quite opposite from men:

Man is the will, and Woman the sentiment. In this ship of humanity, Will
is the rudder, and Sentiment the sail; when Woman affects to steer, the
rudder is only a masked sail. When women engage in any art or trade, it
is usually as a resource, not as a primary object. The life of the affections
is primary to them, so that there is usually no employment or career which
they will not with their own applause and that of society quit for suitable
marriage. And they give entirely to their affections, set their whole for-
tunes on the die, lose themselves eagerly in the glory of their husbands
and children.[28]

Clearly when Emerson wrote "Self-Reliance," he had in mind men,
not women. His views of women were traditional for his time, and
it is not surprising that Edna found no more solace in Emerson
than she did in her father's religion.

   The Awakening is resistant to easy categorization of any kind. A
unique work in American literature, it can only be viewed in many
lights. Seen in terms of the Woman Question, it yields a number
of meanings and insights. Whatever else can be said about it, it
remains a book by a woman about a woman who could not find a
place in the society in which she lived because she was a woman.

NOTES

   1. Per Seyersted, *Kate Chopin: A Critical Biography* (Baton Rouge: Louisiana State University Press, 1969), p. 33. Seyersted states that it was
probably Victoria Claflin who spoke to Chopin.
   2. William Schuyler, "Kate Chopin," *Writer* 7 (August 1894): 115–17,
as quoted in Seyersted, *Kate Chopin*, p. 52.

3. As quoted in ibid., p. 101.

4. Kate Chopin, *The Awakening*, ed. Margaret Culley (1899, rpt. New York: Norton, 1976), p. 6. All further references to this work will be indicated parenthetically within the text.

5. As quoted in Seyersted, *Kate Chopin*, p. 24.

6. See Margaret Fuller, *Woman in the Nineteenth Century* (1845, rpt. New York: Norton, 1971). Fuller wrote, "But that is the very fault of marriage, and of the present relation between the sexes, that the woman does belong to the man instead of forming a whole with him" (p. 176). Charlotte Perkins Gilman expressed a similar idea when she wrote, "Woman's wealth depends on her husband—not on the work she performs." *Women and Economics* (1898, rpt. New York: Harper and Row, 1966), p. 21.

7. Gilman, *Women and Economics*, p. 53.

8. Eble, "A Forgotten Novel: Kate Chopin's *The Awakening*," *Western Humanities Review* 10 (Summer 1956): 261–69, rpt. "A Forgotten Novel," in Chopin, *The Awakening*, ed. Culley, p. 166.

9. George Spangler, "Kate Chopin's *The Awakening*: A Partial Dissent," *Novel* 3 (Spring 1970), 249–55, rpt. "The Ending of the Novel," in Chopin, *The Awakening*, ed. Culley, p. 188.

10. Judith Fryer, *The Faces of Eve: Women in the Nineteenth-Century American Novel* (New York: Oxford University Press, 1976), p. 245.

11. "Books of the Week," *Providence Sunday Journal*, June 4 1899, p. 151; "Books of the Day," Chicago *Times-Herald*, June 1, 1899, p. 9; Frances Porcher, "Kate Chopin's Novel," *Mirror* 9 (May 4, 1899): 6. All of the above are reprinted in Chopin, *The Awakening*, ed. Culley, pp. 149–50.

12. Willa Cather, "Books and Magazines," Pittsburgh *Leader* 8 (July 1899): 6; Signed "Sibert" [Willa Cather], rpt. in Chopin, *The Awakening*, ed. Culley, p. 153.

13. C. L. Deyo, "The Newest Books," *St. Louis Post Dispatch*, May 20, 1899, p. 4, rpt. in Chopin, *The Awakening*, ed. Culley, p. 148.

14. Letter to the Hon. Richard B. Shepard, August 24, 1899, as quoted in Seyersted, *Kate Chopin*, p. 175.

15. Arthur Hobson Quinn, *American Fiction* (New York: Appleton-Century-Crofts, 1936), p. 357.

16. Carlos Baker, *Literary History of the United States*, 3 vols. (New York: Macmillan, 1948), pp. 858–59.

17. Clarence Gohdes, "Exploitation of the Provinces," in *The Literature of the American People*, ed. Arthur Hobson Quinn (New York: Appleton-Century-Crofts, 1951),p. 654.

18. Van Wyck Brooks, *The Confident Years: 1885–1915* (New York: E. P. Dutton, 1952), p. 341.

19. Suzanne Wolkenfield, "Edna's Suicide: The Problem of the One and the Many," in Chopin, *The Awakening*, ed. Culley, p. 223.

20. Jules Chametzky, "Our Decentralized Literature," *Jahrbuch fur Americkstudien* (1972): 56–72, rpt. in Chopin, *The Awakening*, ed. Culley, pp. 200–201.

21. Lawrence Thornton, "The Awakening: A Political Romance," *American Literature* 52 (March 1980): 54.

22. Edmund Wilson, *Patriotic Gore: Studies in the Literature of the American Civil War* (New York: Oxford University Press, 1962), p. 591.

23. Edmund Wilson, Foreword, *The Complete Works of Kate Chopin*, Vol. 1, Introd. Per Seyersted (Baton Rouge: Louisiana State University Press, 1969), p. 14.

24. Lewis Leary, "The Awakening of Kate Chopin," in *Southern Excursions: Essays on Mark Twain and Others* (Baton Rouge: Louisiana State University, 1971), p. 174.

25. Donald Ringe, "Romantic Imagery in Kate Chopin's *The Awakening*," *American Literature* 43 (January 1972): 580–88, rpt. in Chopin, *The Awakening*, ed. Culley, p. 206.

26. Leary, "Awakening of Kate Chopin," p. 170.

27. Eble, "A Forgotten Novel," p. 166; George Arms, "Kate Chopin's *The Awakening* in the Perspective of Her Literary Career," in *Essays on American Literature in Honor of Jay B. Hubbell*, ed. Clarence Gohdes (Durham, N.C.: Duke University Press, 1967), pp. 215–28, rpt. "Contrasting Forces in the Novel," in Culley, p. 177.

28. Ralph Waldo Emerson, "Woman," A Lecture Read Before the Woman's Rights Convention, Boston, September 20, 1855, rpt. in *Miscellanies*, Vol. 11 of *The Complete Works of Ralph Waldo Emerson* (Boston: Houghton Mifflin, 1904), p. 407.

8

Conclusion

THE WRITERS

It is likely that there were so many women writers in the nineteenth century because writing was a career option at a point in time when there were few alternatives for women. While the writers in this study came from the upper middle class, they wrote mainly out of economic need.

All six writers wrote about women's issues, but none made a major commitment to political action. Alcott occasionally lent personal support to suffrage-related causes, and Stowe and Phelps wrote articles about women's rights in addition to their fiction. While others waved the banners for reform, by and large the writers poured their energies into their fiction.

Parental influence was very significant in the lives of at least four of the six women under discussion. Stowe and Phelps were both daughters of Congregational ministers who shared their fathers' desire to instruct, but they used a pen, not a pulpit. Their mothers died young, leaving their daughters only an idealized memory. Both objected to their fathers' stern Calvinist teachings, preferring instead a doctrine of Christian love, which they frequently discussed in their work. Although they lived in the shadow of Andover Theological Seminary, their religion was private, and they wrote out of their own hearts. Sarah Orne Jewett was also greatly influenced by her father, who was not only her mentor but her role

model. The parental influence on Louisa May Alcott is more difficult to ascertain. She loved her mother and pledged herself to help
her with her considerable financial burden, but she clearly both
admired and identified with her formidable father. Her apparently
self-willed death only two days after his suggests the strange bond
that held Bronson and Louisa together.

With the exception of Harriet Beecher Stowe, all the writers discussed in this book made their important literary contributions as
single women. Alcott and Jewett never married. Chopin took up
writing seriously only after the death of her husband. Phelps and
Freeman married when they were in their forties, by which time
they had already written their major works. Only Stowe and Chopin were mothers. Thus in their own lives these women demonstrated the difficulty of combining marriage and career, a problem
often described in their fiction.

Although they shared an interest in the Woman Question, the
extent to which they were influenced by each other or even by
other women writers remains unclear. Stowe, Alcott, and Jewett
were not explicit about literary influences. Although Freeman clearly
felt an affinity for Emily Brontë's work, she vigorously disclaimed
any debt to others. Phelps admired Stowe and felt grateful to Elizabeth Barrett Browning for writing *Aurora Leigh*. Only Chopin explicitly indicated her admiration for American women writers, specifically Jewett and Freeman. If these writers wrote out of a common
tradition, they were not aware of it. It is rather up to us as readers
to make the connections.

CRITICISM

The history of the criticism of each novel from its first publication to the present reveals that the transaction between the reader
and the text is influenced by a variety of cultural factors and expectations. The critics' awareness of the Woman Question is directly related to social conditions of the time. In the late nineteenth
century, as in the present, the Woman Question was a major social
issue, so that at least some readers perceived the exploration of the
issue in fiction, but in the long period following World War I until
the early 1960s, when feminism was rarely discussed, critics fail to
notice the depiction of women's issues in literature.

The question of literary quality is even more esoteric. Different generations have used vastly different criteria, and the standard against which a book is judged is often unclear. Frequently a work that had been hailed as testimony to an author's genius was later dismissed for lack of literary quality.

Nineteenth Century

Four of the six novelists represented here, namely Stowe, Phelps, Jewett, and Freeman, were warmly praised in their time by the critical establishment. The other two, Alcott and Chopin, met with an unfavorable response, but for quite different reasons. Alcott was bypassed as a writer of juveniles, while Chopin was vilified for producing salacious trash. Implicit in nineteenth-century criticism was the belief that a novel should teach morality.

Accordingly, both Stowe and Phelps earned high praise. *Uncle Tom's Cabin* was recognized initially by most critics for its high moral purpose, and its author was commended for her "genius."[1] *The Silent Partner* was not as well received as some works by Phelps, which deliver a more obvious moral message, but it still falls within the parameters of nineteenth-century expectations of morality and was hailed as "effective and artistic," while its author's "genius" was also noted.[2] Freeman and Jewett were duly admired both for their style and for the accuracy of their depictions of New England life.

The critics for the most part paid little attention to subject matter, except in *Uncle Tom's Cabin*, where slavery is clearly the raison d'être for the novel. The authors' concern with the Woman Question was rarely noted. Where such interest was evinced it was generally female critics who felt the issue of sufficient interest to warrant comment. In the rare instances where men noted feminist leanings, they tended to disapprove. The exploration of the Woman Question in *The Silent Partner*, *Work*, and *Pembroke* went entirely unnoticed. Only one critic noted the importance of the Woman Question in *A Country Doctor*. Other critics saw only a minor novel or a "graceful book." Chopin's serious exploration of a woman's desire for independence was generally overlooked by critics who were appalled by what they perceived as its immorality.

No clear notion emerges in nineteenth-century criticism regarding a criterion for literary excellence, nor is there much evidence of an understanding of the female perspective that informs the work.

The Decline of Feminism, 1920–1960

During the roughly forty-year period from the end of World War I to the resurgence of feminism in the 1960s, the novelists in this study were for the most part unnoticed or relegated to minor status. *Uncle Tom's Cabin* was regarded as a period piece, and critics complained of sentimentalism or lack of artistry. But in the 1940s and 1950s, with the emergence of a black consciousness, it again attracted attention. Harriet Beecher Stowe was no longer viewed as a champion of the black cause, but as the perpetrator of a wrong-headed view about the subservient character of blacks.

Critical evaluation of Alcott and Jewett remained fairly consistent through the period. Alcott continued to be regarded mainly as a successful writer of juveniles, while Jewett earned praise as a feminine rather than feminist writer.

The other three writers were notable in the criticism of the period mainly for their absence. Among the few critics who acknowledged Phelps, there was little agreement on the quality of her work. Freeman, when noted at all, was praised for her artistry, while Chopin was almost completely forgotten until Kenneth Eble's 1956 article.

A glance at the college anthologies and literary histories of the period would suggest that the contribution of women writers to American literature was minimal.

The Resurgence of Feminism, 1960 to the Present

With the resurgence of feminism and the advent of feminist criticism, the writers discussed in this book have all attracted renewed interest. While some critics are particularly interested in the feminist doctrine in the works, others are simply more open than previously to the work of women writers.

In the 1960s several critics hailed *Uncle Tom's Cabin* as a work of art, especially because of the subtleties of characterization, which earlier generations had simply failed to note. And by the 1970s feminist critics commented on the women's issues raised in *Uncle*

Tom's Cabin and also insisted on the importance of the novel as literature.

Alcott's novels have likewise been picked up, dusted off, and read with new admiration. Some see Alcott's feminism, but perhaps even more important, virtually all the critics of this period are aware of the female perspective, and seen from that vantage point, the books take on a meaning that was previously lost to critics, though not to Alcott's wide readership.

Phelps and Chopin have attracted renewed interest especially for their feminism. The renascence of Chopin is particularly impressive. No longer put off by what early critics saw as gross immorality, modern critics have found *The Awakening* an extraordinary novel. While feminist critics have focused on the novel's unique feminist statement, other critics have been fascinated by what they perceive as significant parallels with memorable heroines of the time, notably Flaubert's Emma Bovary and James's Isabel Archer.

Jewett and Freeman have been restored to their original position as eminent New England writers who re-created the details of the New England of their time in their fiction. While they are not considered feminist writers, their preoccupation with women and their world has been recognized.

There remains no consistent set of guidelines for establishing the literary value of a work of fiction, but the present generation of critics seems increasingly willing to depart from arbitrary standards of the past.

THE NOVELS

The novels discussed here are about heroines confronting their destinies in a world where the position of women was still a question. We have heard about heroes at least since Aristotle, but heroines are another matter. Aristotle himself maintained that a woman was an inferior subject, and while there were those who persisted in writing about women in spite of Aristotle, there seems to be little agreement about what a heroine is supposed to be.

For some, the term "heroine" conjures up a passive beauty like Cinderella or Sleeping Beauty, whose life is simply a matter of waiting for the handsome prince. Thus, Lee R. Edwards writes about "female heroes" rather than heroines because for her "the hero is a self; the heroine an appendage."[3] She defines heroes as people "whose lives matter because they occupy new territory or suggest alternatives to the cramped dailiness of ordinary existence."[4] When women manage to fit this description, she calls them heroes, in contrast to their weaker sisters, whom she sees as subordinate to men.

While the question of heroinism was raised before the advent of feminist criticism, most of the discussion of heroines began in the 1960s as critics started to reexamine woman-centered novels. The focus of attention has been the nineteenth-century English novel, and there seems little disagreement that a list of heroines in the English novel must include Dorothea Brooke, Emma, Elizabeth Bennet, and Jane Eyre. Susan Seifert calls all of the above "atypical," in contrast to what she perceives to be the stereotypical nineteenth-century heroine, who is "kind, gentle, unhappy, unassertive and intellectually feeble."[5] It is, however, the so-called "atypical heroines" who have captured the interest of the critics. But while the heroine is discussed, the term is rarely defined. In the absence of a definition, the reader can only conclude that while no one seems very sure what a heroine is, heroines are recognized when they appear. And certainly feminist critics seem to have reached similar conclusions about who the heroines of the English novel are.

Rachel Brownstein very simply confesses that heroines are the women characters she read about in her adolescence while safely closeted in the family bathroom. They are the women she knew she would emulate when she escaped from anonymity in the Bronx to become someone special.

Most often she finds that the heroine is the central figure in the marriage plot. "The idea of becoming a heroine," she writes, "marries the female protagonist to the marriage plot, and it marries the woman who reads to fiction."[6] Brownstein goes on to explain that in the "classic English novel" the protagonist realizes her identity when she finds a husband. Thus when Elizabeth Bennet and Emma finally recognize the virtues of Mr. Darcy and Mr. Knightley respectively, they have achieved insight and undeniably will find happiness. Should the heroine make a mistake like Dorothea Brooke, she will suffer. Or perhaps, like Jane Eyre, she will attain a husband only on her own terms and therefore play a more active role in securing her happiness. No matter what the variation, the point is that the heroine marries, and the female reader, at least according to Brownstein, defines herself through the fictitious woman who settles on a husband and thereby realizes her significance.

If Brownstein's explanation is ludicrously far from contemporary hermeneutics, it is, nonetheless, probably accurate. While scholars deconstruct erudite texts, there are probably still untold numbers of adolescent girls who may or may not be hidden away in their parents' bathrooms, but who most assuredly know that Elizabeth, Emma, Dorothea, and Jane are heroines.

When we turn to nineteenth-century American literature written by women, the situation is vastly different. It is hard to imagine adolescent girls hiding in the bathroom to read an American woman's novel, except perhaps *Little Women*, which has survived as a juvenile, while other women's novels have, with the exception of some recent reprints, all but disappeared. Whether, if available, they would have been read with the same fascination as nineteenth-century English novels is impossible to say, but their appeal is quite different.

Certainly the point of the American woman's novel is not to get married. With the possible exception of *Pembroke*, the novels discussed here raise entirely different questions from the English woman's novel of the period. There is no expectation that a woman will realize herself through the selection of an appropriate husband. Rather the question most frequently raised is whether a woman can have marriage and independence, particularly an independent career. The writers who address the issue suggest that this is an impossibility. A choice must be made, and they reject marriage. Female characters in these works often feel that marriage requires subordination of their life interests to men. Thus, they recall Elizabeth Cady Stanton's assertion that marriage is at the heart of the Woman Question.

In *The Silent Partner* and *A Country Doctor* the protagonists refuse their suitors because they see marriage as conflicting with their work. Perley in *The Silent Partner* rejects Maverick because she does not wish to "stunt" herself, and Dr. Leslie in *A Country Doctor* explains that marriage requires a woman to "surrender." The problem is not the individual suitor but marriage itself, as evidenced by Perley's later rejection of Mr. Garrick with the explanation that she has a preference for a business of her own. Similarly, George in *A Country Doctor* must be disappointed, not because he is lacking in manly virtue in any way, but rather because Nan, like Perley, is certain that marriage and career cannot be effectively combined. Sip's refusal of her suitor in *The Silent Partner* indicates that the difficulties posed by marriage for women are not limited to a single class. Like Perley and Nan, Sip sees marriage interfering with her work, and in addition she sees little advantage in bringing children into the oppressive world she has experienced; rather the world must be reformed before marriage and childbearing can be acceptable life options.

In *The Awakening* and *Work* the issue for the female protagonist is not focused on a specific career, but there is again a fear that marriage destroys independence by forcing women to play a subordinate role in return for economic security. Edna in *The Awakening* gives up the luxuries of her marriage in her effort for independence, while in *Work* Christie turns down Mr. Fletcher's proposal despite her desire for the material comforts that his money might provide her. Both women believe that marriage must be based on love, not money, but for different reasons love does not last. When Edna's lover leaves her and Christie's husband is killed in the war, each must face life alone. Thus, while the possibility of lasting love is raised, in neither novel is it brought to fruition.

Still other parallels emerge in view of marriage presented in *Pembroke*, *Uncle Tom's Cabin*, and *Work*. In each of these novels there are wives who are intellectually and morally superior to their husbands, and so they endeavor to govern their husbands in whatever way they can. In *Pembroke* Cephas Barnard, Silas Berry, and Caleb Thayer, the generation of middle-aged fathers, are all weak and foolish men; their wives attempt to instruct them but often must satisfy themselves by commiserating with other women. Similarly, in *Uncle Tom's Cabin* the lifework of Mrs. Shelby and Mrs. Bird, both exemplary women, is to teach their husbands to be better. This will also become Eliza's task when she and George are at last reunited. The pattern persists in *Work*, where Aunt Betsey and Cynthia Wilkins devote themselves to inferior men whom they hope to improve.

Despite overwhelming social and economic pressure for women

to marry in the nineteenth century, unmarried women in the novels are generally portrayed as admirable and/or happy in their life choices. In *Uncle Tom's Cabin* Miss Ophelia and Cassy refuse to succumb to individual men or to an institution created by men and thereby achieve their own goals and exercise power over others. And at the end of *The Silent Partner* and *A Country Doctor*, the protagonists are described as very happy in their choice of spinsterhood. Similarly the conclusion of *Work* finds Christie joyfully engaged with other women to build a new future.

Chopin and Freeman remain ambivalent about the possibility of a woman's finding happiness either alone or in marriage. In *The Awakening*, when Edna rejects as role models both Mlle. Reisz, the single artist, and Mme. Ratignolle, the archetype mother, she remains unable to find a viable place in the world. Freeman shows multiple examples of women and sweethearts devoting themselves to men unworthy of their efforts and yet never suggests that a woman might find satisfaction alone. The economic benefit of marriage is underscored by Sylvia's timely rescue on the way to the poorhouse, but if marriage affords benefits other than economic, these are not shown in the novel.

When marriage is rejected, other options are inevitably raised. Elizabeth Cady Stanton and Victoria Woodhull warned that free love was at the heart of the women's rights movement. The vituperation Kate Chopin had to face as a result of her handling of this subject points out the difficulty confronted by a writer wishing to discuss the question of female sexuality. Nonetheless, three of the six writers do at least broach the subject. For Chopin sexual liberation is an essential part of woman's total freedom, but Edna, like other nineteenth-century heroines, finds death, not happiness. She is punished, as were Madame Bovary and Anna Karenina. There is apparently no way for a woman of the time to exercise sexual freedom and maintain a place in the social fabric.

Stowe introduces the issue of free love in *Uncle Tom's Cabin* when she makes the point that Cassy willingly gave herself to her first master because she loved him, a detail which would seem to be gratuitous unless Stowe wished to confront the question of romantic or sexual love outside of marriage. Cassy is, of course, black, so that she is not confined within the same social conventions that limit the behavior of white people. Nonetheless, like Edna, she suffers for her behavior when the man she loves ultimately leaves her.

In *Pembroke* sexual freedom also leads to misery. When Rebecca becomes pregnant and is forced to marry William hastily, the wedding takes place in, of all places, the home of the village whore. The baby conceived out of wedlock dies, as if to provide retribution for the sin of its parents. Sexual freedom seems inevitably to result in punishment, especially for women. If nineteenth-century marriage was unsatisfactory, the novels suggest that love outside of marriage was not a reasonable alternative. In a society where the Puritan influence remained strong, women would have to find fulfillment in other ways.

In the novels under discussion, work—even domestic work—is given a very high priority as a means by which women assert independence and express individuality. Both Harriet Beecher Stowe and Mary Wilkins Freeman elevate women's domestic work. In *Uncle Tom's Cabin* Mrs. Shelby, Miss Ophelia, and Rachel Halliday, the women who perform domestic tasks competently, are expected to earn our highest regard, while there is obvious contempt for Marie St. Claire, who lolls about complaining of "sick headaches." In *Pembroke* it is made clear that men need women to perform the important domestic work that makes life pleasant and comfortable. Barney Thayer lives in bachelor misery when he rejects Charlotte, and Cephas Barnard cannot bake an edible pie. Louisa May Alcott does not glorify domestic work as do Stowe and Freeman, but she maintains a consistent view that all work, including domestic, is an important means to independence and self-respect.

In *The Awakening*, *A Country Doctor*, and *The Silent Partner* women seek fulfillment in professional work and in so doing are forced to deny the expectations of those around them that such work is unsuitable for women. In *The Awakening* Edna's desire to be an artist is in part a rebellion against her husand's denial of her right to work at a task unrelated to the household. Edna's inability to find satisfaction in her painting is part of her larger failure at self-definition. Nan in *A Country Doctor* and Perley in *The Silent Partner* are more fortunate in that they find happiness in the work they chose and succeed in proving to those who oppose their efforts that they are supremely competent in their professions.

In attempting to define her own destiny, the American heroine rejects patriarchal assumptions not only about marriage and work but also about religion, which was often used as the justification for women's inferior position. Stowe, Phelps, Alcott, and Chopin all reject the religion of their fathers. The most radical departure from orthodoxy is found in *Uncle Tom's Cabin*, where a girl becomes a Christ figure. In addition, the church is repudiated several times in the novel because ministers uphold slavery, which Stowe sees as a direct contradiction to the doctrine of love preached by Jesus. Phelps's rebellion against orthodoxy may be compared to that of Stowe in that the true religion is embodied in a woman. When Sip becomes a preacher she criticizes "rich religion," a notion which is reminiscent of Stowe, who describes the "piety" of Marie St. Claire as it is reflected in the finery she wears when she attends church. Both Stowe and Phelps emphasize that the doctrine of love is at the heart of real religion.

Louisa May Alcott also found herself at odds with formal religion. Christie, alone and depressed, is unable to obtain the solace she seeks in religion until she finds the free church of Mr. Powers. Finally, Edna's rebellion in *The Awakening* includes a rejection of her father's "gloomy Presbyterianism." When she later feels alienated in a Catholic church, it becomes clear that it is not a particular religious creed but rather religion itself which has become irrelevant.

As women increasingly rebelled against the beliefs and requirements of a patriarchy they did not create, it is not surprising that they were often in the forefront of the reform movement, especially as they saw implications for women's rights.

Stowe, Alcott, and Phelps were among those who felt that women should lead in the effort for greater social equality. For Stowe abolition was a woman's issue, which she avidly supported in *Uncle Tom's Cabin* and *Dred*. But once abolition became a reality, she turned her efforts for the next several years directly to the cause of women's rights.

Perhaps even more than Stowe, Phelps underscores the connection between women's rights and the rights of other disadvantaged groups. Perley is motivated to act on behalf of the factory workers because, like them, she has been unjustly denied her rights by the partners. In refusing to allow Perley to participate in running the factory on the grounds that she is a woman, the partners exhibit the same lack of understanding that they show the factory workers. Like Stowe, Phelps advocates the cause of all the oppressed, regardless of sex, but she is particularly sensitive to the way in which male-dominated institutions victimize women. Thus, Stowe emphasizes the plight of the slave mother, while Phelps focuses on the woman factory worker through her depiction of the substandard conditions under which Sip lives.

Alcott's view is narrower than that of either Stowe or Phelps. Her concern is the woman worker, whom she shows throughout the novel as underpaid, undervalued, and severely limited in work options. When Christie chooses as her lifework the emancipation of women, her first act is to assist the workers, for she sees them as the most disadvantaged group.

While Sarah Orne Jewett and Kate Chopin were far less politically aware than Stowe, Alcott, or Phelps, both writers interject the question of women's rights as it directly relates to the protagonists' lives. Nan in *A Country Doctor* often laments the fact that she is denied the opportunities given to boys and men, thus indicating that her problem is a question of women's rights. In *The Awakening* it is not Edna but her husband who actually articulates the idea of women's rights. As noted earlier, he suggests that underneath her discontent is "some sort of notion in her head about the eternal rights of women."[7]

The only writer in this study who does not directly or indirectly discuss the rights of women is Freeman. The issue does not surface because in the microcosm of *Pembroke* women carve out a position superior to that of men. Insulated in their matriarchal community, neither men nor women concern themselves with larger issues of reform.

In rejecting prevailing views about marriage, work, and religion, writers were challenging the power structure in American society. In five of the six novels, women demonstrate power over their own destinies and/or those of others. Female power is explained by psychologist David McClelland as fundamentally different from male power. McClelland asserts, "a woman's behavior is shaped by role expectations rooted in history and in society, and power motivation expresses itself in terms of how women are expected to behave."[8] Thus a woman may exert power through her role as nurturer or mother. Stowe, Phelps, and Alcott are all reformers who see the possibility of a better world when women exercise power through love.

In *Uncle Tom's Cabin* women attempt to rule men by inculcating in them motherly values of love and compassion. Even when men deny their mothers and live less than admirable lives, they remain in their mothers' power. St. Claire's dying word is "Mother." And when Cassy frightens Legree by wearing a white sheet he perceives as his mother's shroud, he falls into a swoon and apparently never recovers from his torment. Although mothers do not exercise their power directly, Stowe's notion is that the world will be a better place when men finally live in accord with their mothers' teachings.

Phelps, like Stowe, suggests that the world would function more efficiently were women's values permitted to prevail. When Perley succeeds where the male partners fail in averting a strike, she proves that a woman can exercise effective leadership through love and understanding. Sip likewise extends love and thereby becomes a charismatic preacher. Thus women prove that in both business and the ministry they can be more effective than men by substituting love for aggression.

For Alcott the issue is not women exercising power over men, but rather women enhancing their own power through loving comradeship. Thus the hope for the future lies in women joined in mutual love to accomplish the tasks of the future.

Freeman and Jewett lack a social vision, but each maintains her own version of woman's power. Freeman, like Stowe, emphasizes motherly values. Barnaby in his sickness remembers Charlotte and longs for "the maternal and protecting element of her love."[9] And Rebecca holds William in her arms as though he were "a hurt child."[10] Hannah Berry claims that Barney Thayer and Cephas Barnard are "just like two little boys."[11] It remains for the women to love them and care for them so that, like Barney at the end of the novel, they can put aside their deformities.

Jewett's position is closer to that of Alcott in that she shows that women are able to govern their own lives separately from men. When George Gerry watches Nan set a man's shoulder, he feels "weak and womanish" and worries that Nan does not need his protection.[12] Nan's actions in effect upset the social order which pre-

sumes that men must care for women. Male authority apparently
vanishes when women prove that they do not need such care.

Only Chopin fails to present a view of woman's power. While
Edna rejects patriarchal authority, she fails to find power within
herself to control either her own life or that of others. Hers is a
failure of the individual will.

The independent woman who challenges the power structure bears
little resemblance to her counterpart in the English novel. Her an-
alogue is rather with her American brother, the hero of classic
American literature, the adventurer. But nineteenth-century wom-
en's novels have not been recognized as adventure stories; rather
they are generally classified under the rubric "domestic novels."
Among writers in this book the term has been applied especially to
the work of Stowe, Alcott, and Freeman. But while it is an accurate designation, it is pejorative and of limited use in understanding
the novels. We could, for example, say that *Moby Dick* is a story
about whaling, but having stated that we would be recognizing
only the milieu which forms the context of the novel while ignoring
its meaning. In the same way that Melville explored life's complex-
ities in the world of a whaling vessel, women novelists often viewed
life's conflicts among the pots and pans and bric-a-brac of a world
familiar to them. Nevertheless, the subject of the novels is not domestic detail any more than Melville's real subject is whales. It is
instead the motivations and conflicts of the characters that engage
us because we recognize the universal problems of the human heart,
which transcend male and female.

Nonetheless, American critics have continued to ignore both
nineteenth-century women's novels and feminist criticism in insist-
ing on the masculinity of America's literary tradition. For example,
George Stade and Martin Green in recent analyses describe American literature as primarily concerned with adventure stories from
which women are excluded. Stade maintains that the American novel
until recently has dealt with the "opposition . . . between women
and adventure," while Green calls the adventure story "the central
achievement of American literature." Like Stade, he assumes that
the adventure story is a male genre:

the adventure tale was written almost exclusively for a masculine audience.
It has been the main literary means by which males have been taught to

take initiatives, to run risks, to give orders, to fight defeat and dominate; while females have been taught, both by being ignored by the genre and being reduced to passive roles within it, *not* to do those things.[13]

If we accept Green's definition, then the novels discussed here might be considered female adventure stories. The female protagonists are not passive creatures who are willing *not* to do things. On the contrary, they most certainly take initiatives, run risks, give orders, and sometimes even fight, defeat, and dominate. To be sure, they do all this in a vastly different context than men, but they do it nonetheless, and in so doing become heroines. In other words, male novels which reject civilization for nature and female novels which take place in the confines of society may not be as different as has been supposed.

Differences in novels written by men and women in nineteenth-century America stem largely from the fact that women generally write women-centered novels while men write men-centered novels. There are, of course, notable exceptions, but leaving those aside, some obvious conclusions can be drawn. To a large extent writers must write out of personal experience and must create characters who are limited to the possibilities available to their sex. It would, therefore, be as unlikely for a woman in the nineteenth century to write about rafting on the Mississippi or life on a whaling ship as it would be for a man to write about baking pies or kneading dough, activities described in *Pembroke* and *Work* respectively.[14] Thus, plot, setting, and iconography may be substantially different when we compare the novels written by men and women. Nonetheless, certain themes are frequently reiterated regardless of the gender of the writer. We find the same urge to break with tradition, the same rejection of conventional values, and the same desire for adventure.

Four of the six novels analyzed in this book have an adventurous heroine at their center: Perley in *The Silent Partner*, Christie in *Work*, Nan in *A Country Doctor*, and Edna in *The Awakening*. The first three heroines overcome obstacles to secure their goals and in so doing resist the interference of men, who assume they need their assistance or guidance. Perley and Nan, in rejecting marriage and opting for careers that are not ordinarily open to women, must fight their communities, which insist that women should not pursue careers which are thought to be men's prerogatives. But each woman rejects the many voices raised around her and pursues her goals irrespective of the unconventionality of her choice. They are not afraid to isolate themselves from men or other women as they decide to be different.

Christie, like Perley and Nan, also asserts independence in the area of work, but it is in the act of working, not in the nature of the job. While Christie's jobs are domestic, she is individualistic insofar as she chooses work over marriage until she finally meets the man she loves. Even then, he is not her destiny, as a man so often is in the English novel. Rather he is incidental to the plot, and she realizes her goals on her own. As she moves from job to job, she rejects female role models and becomes her own person. Her intention is to create a new world in which she will not play a traditional female role.

Edna is a very different kind of heroine because she does not triumph. Her effort to take the initiative and run risks leads to death; nevertheless, her aspirations to create a new life set her apart from conventional womanhood. In her death she rejects the destiny that had been assigned to her.

Since *Uncle Tom's Cabin* and *Pembroke* are novels with multiple plots and many female characters, it is difficult to isolate a heroine. Nonetheless, both Stowe and Freeman give us versions of the heroic woman. In *Uncle Tom's Cabin* the black women, Eliza and Cassy, embody the heroic. Both women risk their lives to achieve their ends over the cruel white slave-traders who dominate the patriarchy in which they live. But they differ from heroes in their motivation. They undertake their heroic flights to freedom to save the children, whose lives they value more than their own. Thus they exhibit love and altruism, which is not ordinarily part of the heroic mode.

Although there are many women characters in *Pembroke*, Charlotte Barnard alone seems worthy of the designation "heroine" because of her willingness to take the initiative and run risks. She does not wait for Barney to select her, but she goes to him in his time of need despite the disapproval of the neighborhood gossips. As a result she wins him on her own terms. If her goal is conventional, her method of achieving it is not. She too breaks the rules in asserting her independence.

Thus, in American literature a heroine emerges who is independent and fearless. She operates within a conventional context, generally not moving very far from home, but like her American brother, she is willing to be different even if she must remain alone and face the disapproval of others. Compared to her English counterpart, she is realistic rather than romantic. She is not necessarily beautiful like most British heroines, nor is she generally the object of men's desires. But she has a strength and a purpose that are frequently denied in her sex.

While each of the novels explores the Woman Question from a unique perspective, all of them suggest the rejection of the ideal of True Womanhood in favor of greater freedom and eq'*ality for women. In each novel there is an attempt to redefine woman's position so that in some way she is free to be herself instead of being subjected to the will of her husband or to larger patriarchal society. If the women's magazines still advocated a submissive womanhood, these novelists above all denied that view. There was no single description of the New Woman, but there seemed to be a consensus that she would control her own destiny in a way as yet only partially defined.

NOTES

1. Lee R. Edwards, "The Labor of Psyche: Toward a Theory of Female Heroism," *Critical Inquiry* 6 (1979): 47, 48.

2. Ibid., p. 77.

3. Ibid., p. 36.

4. Ibid.,p. 33.

5. Susan Siefert, *The Dilemma of the Talented Heroine: A Study in Nineteenth-Century Fiction* (Montreal: Eden, 1977), Preface.

6. Rachel M. Brownstein, *Becoming a Heroine: Reading About Women in Novels* (New York: Viking, 1982), p. xvi.

7. Kate Chopin, *The Awakening*, ed. Margaret Culley (1899, rpt. New York: Norton, 1976), p. 65.

8. David C. McClelland, *Power: The Inner Experience* (New York: Irvington, 1975), pp. 93–94.

9. Mary Wilkins Freeman, *Pembroke* (1894, rpt. New York: Harper, 1899), p. 316.

10. Ibid., p. 143.

11. Ibid., p. 42.

12. Sarah Orne Jewett, *A Country Doctor* (Boston: Houghton Mifflin, 1884), p. 266.

13. George Stade, "Men, Boys and Wimps," *New York Times Book Review*, August 12, 1984, p. 1; Martin Green, *The Great American Adventure* (Boston: Beacon Press, 1984), pp. 1–2.

14. Judith Fetterley makes the point that women did frequently accompany their husbands on whaling ships, but the experience of whaling was, nonetheless, a male experience. See *Provisions: A Reader from Nineteenth-Century American Women* (Bloomington: Indiana University Press, 1985), p. 28.

Bibliography

LITERATURE: PRIMARY SOURCES

Alcott, Louisa May [A. M. Barnard, pseud.]. "Behind a Mask; or, A Woman's Power." In *Behind a Mask: The Unknown Thrillers of Louisa May Alcott*. Edited by Madeline Stern. New York: William Morrow, 1975, pp. 1–104.

———. "Cupid and Chow-Chow." In *Aunt Jo's Scrapbag*, Vol. III. Boston: Roberts Brothers, 1896, pp. 1–40.

———. *Little Women*. 1868–1869. Introduction by Madelon Bedell. New York: Modern Library, 1983.

———. *Work: A Story of Experience*. 1873. Introduction by Sarah Elbert. New York: Schocken, 1977.

Chopin, Kate. *The Awakening*. 1899. Rpt. as *The Awakening: An Authoritative Text, Contexts, Criticism*. Edited by Margaret Culley. New York: W. W. Norton, 1976.

Freeman, Mary Wilkins. "Good Wits, Pen and Paper." In *What Women Can Earn*. Edited by G. H. Dodge et al. New York, 1899, pp. 28–29.

———. *Pembroke*. New York: Harper, 1899.

Jewett, Sarah Orne. *A Country Doctor*. Boston: Houghton Mifflin, 1884.

———. *The Country of the Pointed Firs*. 1896. Rpt. in *Short Fiction of Sarah Orne Jewett and Mary Wilkins Freeman*. Edited by Barbara H. Solomon. New York: New American Library, 1979, pp. 47–151.

———. "Tom's Husband." *Atlantic Monthly* 49 (February 1882): 205–13.

———. "A White Heron." In *Deephaven and Other Stories*. Edited by Richard Cary. New Haven: College and University Press, 1966, pp. 202–12.

Phelps, Elizabeth Stuart. *Austin Phelps*. New York: Scribner's, 1891.

———. *Chapters from a Life*. Boston: Houghton Mifflin, 1896.

———. "The Higher Claim." *Independent* 23 (October 5, 1871): 1.

———. *The Silent Partner*. 1871. Rpt. in *The Silent Partner and "The Tenth of January."* Afterword by Mari Jo Buhle and Florence Howe. Old Westbury, N.Y.: Feminist Press, 1983.

———. "The True Woman." *Independent* 23 (October 19, 1871): 1.

———. "What Shall They Do?" *Harper's New Monthly* 35 (September 1867): 519–23.

———. "Women and Money." *Independent* 23 (August 14, 1871): 1.

Stowe, Harriet Beecher. *Household Papers and Stories*. Boston: Houghton Mifflin, 1896.

———. *The Key to Uncle Tom's Cabin*. Boston: John B. Jewett, 1854.

———. *Lady Byron Vindicated*. Boston: Fields, Osgood, 1870.

———. *My Wife and I*. New York: J. B. Ford, 1871.

———. *Pink and White Tyranny*. 1871. Rpt. in *Poganuc People and Pink and White Tyranny*. Boston: Houghton Mifflin, 1899, pp. 267–523.

———. *Uncle Tom's Cabin; or, Life Among the Lowly*. 1852. Introduction by Ann Douglas. New York: Penguin, 1981.

———. *We and Our Neighbors*. 1875. Boston: Houghton Mifflin, 1900.

———. "What Will You Do With Her? or, The Woman Question." In *Household Papers and Stories*. Boston: Houghton Mifflin, 1896, pp. 231–48.

———. "Woman's Sphere." In *Household Papers and Stories*. Boston: Houghton Mifflin, 1896, pp. 249–73.

CRITICISM AND REFERENCES

Abernathy, J. N. "The Womanliness of Literary Women." *Lippincott's* 55 (April 1895): 570.

Adams, John R. *Harriet Beecher Stowe*. New York: Twayne, 1963.

Ammons, Elizabeth, ed. *Critical Essays on Harriet Beecher Stowe*. Boston: G. K. Hall, 1980.

Anthony, Katherine. *Louisa May Alcott*. 1938. Westport, Conn.: Greenwood Press, 1977.

Ashton, Jean. *Harriet Beecher Stowe: A Reference Guide*. Boston: G. K. Hall, 1977.

Auerbach, Nina. Afterword. *Little Women*, by Louisa May Alcott. New York: Bantam, 1983, pp. 461–70.

Baym, Nina. *Woman's Fiction: A Guide to Novels by and About Women in America, 1820–1970*. Ithaca, N.Y.: Cornell University Press, 1978.

Bedell, Madelon. Introduction. *Little Women*, by Louisa May Alcott. New York: Modern Library, 1983, pp. ix–xlix.

Beer, Thomas. *The Mauve Decade: American Life at the End of the Century*. Garden City, N.J.: Garden City Publishing, 1926.

Bennett, Mary Angela. "Elizabeth Stuart Phelps." Diss., University of Pennsylvania, 1939.

Berthoff, Warner. *The Ferment of Realism: American Literature 1844–1919*. New York: Free Press, 1965.

Bettelheim, Bruno. *The Uses of Enchantment: The Meaning and Importance of Fairy Tales*. New York: Vintage, 1977.

Brooks, Van Wyck. *The Confident Years: 1885–1915*. New York: Dutton, 1952.

———. *New England: Indian Summer, 1865–1915*. New York: Dutton, 1940.

Brophy, Brigid. "Sentimentality and Louisa May Alcott." *New York Times Book Review*, December 1964. Rpt. in *Don't Never Forget: Collected Views and Reviews*. New York: Holt, Rinehart, 1966, pp. 113–20.

Brownstein, Rachel M. *Becoming a Heroine: Reading About Women in Novels*. New York: Viking, 1982.

Buchan, A. M. *"Our Dear Sarah": An Essay on Sarah Orne Jewett*. New Series Language and Literature, no. 24. St. Louis: Washington University Studies, 1953.

Cary, Richard. *Sarah Orne Jewett*. New York: Twayne, 1962.

———, ed. *Appreciation of Sarah Orne Jewett: 29 Interpretive Essays*. Waterville, Me.: Colby College Press, 1973.

———, ed. *Sarah Orne Jewett Letters*. Waterville, Me.: Colby College Press, 1956.

Cather, Willa. Preface. *The Best Short Stories of Sarah Orne Jewett*, by Sarah Orne Jewett. 2 vols. Boston: Houghton Mifflin, 1925, 1:ix–xix.

Cheney, Edna, ed. *Louisa May Alcott, Her Life, Letters, and Journals*. Boston: Roberts Brothers, 1897.

Chesterton, G. K. "Louisa Alcott." In *A Handful of Authors: Essays on Books and Writers*. 1953. New York: Holt, Rinehart, 1966. 163–68.

Rev. of *A Country Doctor*, by Sarah Orne Jewett. *Atlantic Monthly* 54 (September 1884): 418–19.

Cowie, Alexander. *The Rise of the American Novel*. New York: Appleton, Century, 1951.

Cross, Barbara M. "Stowe, Harriet Beecher." In *Notable American Women, 1607–1950*. Cambridge, Mass.: Belknap Press, 1971.

Crozier, Alice C. *The Novels of Harriet Beecher Stowe*. New York: Oxford University Press, 1969.

Rev. of *Dr. Warrick's Daughters*, by Rebecca Harding Davis. *Harper's New Monthly* 92 (April 1896). Rpt. in *Harper's Lost Reviews*. Edited by Clayton L. Eichelberger. Millwood, N.J.: KTO Press, 1976, p. 501.

Donovan, Josephine. *Sarah Orne Jewett*. New York: Frederick Ungar, 1980.

Edwards, Lee R. "The Labor of Psyche: Toward a Theory of Female Heroism." *Critical Inquiry* 6 (1979): 33–63.

Edwards, Lee R., and Arlyn Diamond. Introduction. *American Voices, American Women*. New York: Avon, 1973, pp. 11–18.

Elbert (Diamant), Sarah. "Louisa May Alcott and the Woman Problem." Diss., Cornell University, 1974.

Ellman, Mary. "Phallic Criticism." In *Thinking About Women*. New York: Harcourt Brace Jovanovich, 1968. Rpt. in *Women's Liberation and Literature*. Edited by Elaine Showalter. New York: Harcourt Brace Jovanovich, 1971, pp. 213–22.

Fetterley, Judith, ed. *Provisions: A Reader from 19th-Century American Women*. Bloomington: Indiana University Press, 1985.

————. *The Resisting Reader: A Feminist Approach to American Fiction*. Bloomington: Indiana University Press, 1978.

Fiedler, Leslie. *Love and Death in the American Novel*. New York: Stein & Day, 1966.

Foster, Charles H. *The Rungless Ladder: Harriet Beecher Stowe and New England Puritanism*. Durham, N.C.: Duke University Press, 1954.

Foster, Edward. *Mary E. Wilkins Freeman*. New York: Hendricks House, 1956.

Frost, John Eldridge. *Sarah Orne Jewett*. Milford, N.H.: Cabinet Press, 1960.

Fryer, Judith. *The Faces of Eve: Women in the Nineteenth-Century American Novel*. New York: Oxford University Press, 1976.

Gilbert, Sandra, and Susan Gubar. *The Madwoman in the Attic: The Woman Writer and the Nineteenth-Century Literary Imagination*. New Haven: Yale University Press, 1979.

Hart, John S. *The Female Prose Writers of America*. Philadelphia: E. H. Butler, 1857.

Rev. of *Hedged In*, by Elizabeth Stuart Phelps. *Atlantic Monthly* 25 (1870): 756–57.

Hicks, Granville. *The Great Tradition*. New York: Macmillan, 1933.

Higginson, Thomas Wentworth. *Short Studies of American Authors*. 1877. New York: Longmans, 1966.

Howells, William Dean. "Editor's Study." *Harper's New Monthly* 74 (1877), 482–86.

————. *Life in Letters of William Dean Howells*, Vol. II. Edited by Mildred Howells. New York: Doubleday, 1928.

——. *My Literary Passions*. Library Edition of the *Writings of William Dean Howells*. New York: Harper, 1895.

James, Henry. "Mr. and Mrs. Fields." *Cornhill Magazine* 39 (July 1915): 29–43, rpt. (with minor correction of Henry James's New England geography) in *Atlantic Monthly* 116 (July 1915): 21–31.

——. *A Small Boy and Others*. New York: Charles Scribner's, 1913.

Kelly, Lori Dunin. *Life and Works of Elizabeth Stuart Phelps: Victorian Feminist Writer*. Troy, N.Y.: Whitston, 1983.

Kessler, Carol Farley. *Elizabeth Stuart Phelps*. Boston: Twayne, 1982.

Kimball, Gayle. *The Religious Ideas of Harriet Beecher Stowe: Her Gospel of Womanhood*. New York: Edwin Mellen Press, 1982.

Lauter, Paul, ed. *Reconstructing American Literature: Courses, Syllabi, Issues*. Old Westbury, N.Y.: Feminist Press, 1983.

Leary, Lewis. "The Awakening of Kate Chopin." In *Southern Excursions: Essays on Mark Twain and Others*. Baton Rouge: Louisiana State University Press, 1971, pp. 159–75.

Lewisohn, Ludwig. *Expression in America*. New York: Harper, 1932.

Lynn, Kenneth. "Harriet Beecher Stowe." In *Visions of America*. Westport, Conn.: Greenwood Press, 1973, pp. 27–48.

McClelland, David C. *Power: The Inner Experience*. New York: Irvington, 1975.

Machen, Arthur. *Hieroglyphics*. 1902. London: Unicorn Press, 1960.

Macy, John. "The Passing of the Yankee." *Bookman* 73 (1931): 616–21.

——. ed. *American Writers on American Literature*. New York: Horace Liveright, 1931.

Marsella, Joy A. *The Promise of Destiny: Children and Women in the Short Stories of Louisa May Alcott*. Westport, Conn.: Greenwood Press, 1983.

Matthiessen, Francis Otto. *The American Renaissance*. New York: Oxford University Press, 1941.

——. *Sarah Orne Jewett*. Boston: Houghton Mifflin, 1929.

Moers, Ellen. *Harriet Beecher Stowe and American Literature*. Hartford, Conn.: Stowe-Day, 1978.

——. *Literary Women*. 1963. Garden City, N.Y.: Anchor, 1977.

Morgan, Ellen. "The Atypical Woman: Nan Prince in the Literary Transition to Feminism." *Kate Chopin Newsletter* 2 (Fall 1976): 33–37.

Overton, Grant Martin. *The Women Who Make Our Novels*. New York: Moffat, Yard, 1918.

Parrington, Vernon. *Main Currents in American Thought*. New York: Harcourt, Brace, 1927–1930.

Pattee, Fred Lewis. *Development of the American Short Story*. New York: Harper, 1923.

——. *The Feminine Fifties*. 1940. New York: Kennikat Press, 1960.

———. *A History of American Literature Since 1870*. New York: Cooper Square, 1915.

———. "On the Terminal Moraine of New England Puritanism." In *Side-Lights on American Literature*. New York: Century, 1922, pp. 175–209.

Payne, Alma. *Louisa May Alcott, a Reference Guide*. Boston: G. K. Hall, 1980.

Perry, Bliss. *A Study of Prose Fiction*. Cambridge, Mass.: Riverside Press, 1902.

Quinn, Arthur Hobson. *American Fiction: An Historical and Critical Survey*. New York: Appleton-Century-Crofts, 1936.

———. *The Literature of the American People*. New York: Appleton-Century-Crofts, 1951.

Rankin, Daniel S. *Kate Chopin and Her Creole Stories*. Philadelphia: University of Pennsylvania Press, 1932.

Saxton, Martha. *Louisa May: A Modern Biography of Louisa May Alcott*. Boston: Houghton Mifflin, 1977.

Seyersted, Per. *Kate Chopin: A Critical Biography*. Baton Rouge: Louisiana State University Press, 1969.

Rev. of *The Silent Partner*, by Elizabeth Stuart Phelps. *Harper's New Monthly* 43 (1871): 300–301.

Rev. of *The Silent Partner*, by Elizabeth Stuart Phelps. *Literary World* 1 (1871): 165–67.

Solomon, Barbara. Introduction. *Short Fiction of Sarah Orne Jewett and Mary Wilkins Freeman*. New York: New American Library, 1979, pp. 1–42.

Spiller, Robert, et al. *Literary History of the United States*. 3 vols. New York: Macmillan, 1948.

Stade, George. "Men, Boys and Wimps." *New York Times Book Review*, 12 August 1984, pp. 1, 22–23.

Stansell, Christine. "Woman: An Issue." *Massachusetts Review* 13 (1972): 239–56.

Stern, Madeline. Introduction. *Behind a Mask: The Unknown Thrillers of Louisa May Alcott*. New York: William Morrow, 1975, pp. vii–xxv.

———. *Louisa May Alcott*. Norman: University of Oklahoma Press, 1950.

———, ed. *Critical Essays on Louisa May Alcott*. Boston: G. K. Hall, 1984.

Rev. of *The Story of Avis*, by Elizabeth Stuart Phelps. *Harper's New Monthly* 56 (1878): 310.

Thompson, Charles M. "Miss Wilkins: An Idealist in Masquerade." *Atlantic Monthly* 83 (1899): 665–75.

Thornton, Lawrence. "*The Awakening: A Political Romance*." *American Literature* 52 (1980): 50–66.

Rev. of *Uncle Tom's Cabin*, by Harriet Beecher Stowe. *Blackwood's Edinburgh Magazine* 74 (1853): 393–424.

Rev. of *Uncle Tom's Cabin*, by Harriet Beecher Stowe. *North American Review* 77 (October 1853): 466–67.

Wagenknecht, Edward. *Harriet Beecher Stowe: The Known and the Unknown.* New York: Oxford University Press, 1965.

Warner, Sylvia Townsend. "Item, One Empty House." *New Yorker*, 26 March 1966, pp. 131–38.

Westbrook, Perry D. *Acres of Flint: Sarah Orne Jewett and Her Contemporaries.* Metuchen, N.J.: Scarecrow, 1981.

———. *Mary Wilkins Freeman.* New York: Twayne, 1967.

Williams, Blanche Colton. *Our Short Story Writers.* New York: Dodd, Mead, 1926.

Wilson, Edmund. Foreword. *The Complete Works of Kate Chopin*, vol. 1. Introduction by Per Seyersted. Baton Rouge: Louisiana State University Press, 1969, pp. 13–15.

———. *Patriotic Gore: Studies in the Literature of the American Civil War.* New York: Oxford University Press, 1962.

Wilson, Forrest. *Crusader in Crinoline.* New York: J. B. Lippincott, 1941.

Woolf, Virginia. *A Room of One's Own.* New York: Harcourt, Brace, 1929.

Rev. of *Work*, by Louisa May Alcott. *Harper's New Monthly Magazine* 47 (September 1873), 614–15.

Ziff, Larzer. *The American 1890's: Life and Times of a Lost Generation.* New York: Viking, 1966.

HISTORY OF THE WOMAN QUESTION

Allan, Nathan. "The Other Side of the Question." *Nation* 5 (1867): 316.

Beard, Mary R. *Woman as Force in History.* New York: Macmillan, 1947.

Beecher, Catherine E., and Harriet Beecher Stowe. *The American Woman's Home: Or Principles of Domestic Science.* New York: J. B. Ford, 1869.

Blake, Nelson Manfred. *The Road to Reno: A History of Divorce in the United States.* New York: Macmillan, 1962.

Bloomer, D. C. *Life and Writings of Amelia Bloomer.* New York: Schocken, 1975.

Buhle, Mari Jo, and Paul Buhle. *The Concise History of Woman Suffrage.* Urbana: University of Illinois, 1978.

Cross, Barbara M., ed. *The Educated Woman in America: Selected Writings of Catherine Beecher, Margaret Fuller, and M. Carey Thomas.* New York: Teachers College Press, 1965.

Douglas, Ann. *The Feminization of American Culture.* New York: Knopf, 1977.

Emerson, Ralph Waldo. "Woman." A Lecture Read Before the Woman's Rights Convention, Boston, September 20, 1855. Rpt. in *Miscellanies*. Vol. 11 of *The Complete Works of Ralph Waldo Emerson*. Boston: Houghton, Mifflin, 1904, p. 407.

Flexner, Eleanor. *Century of Struggle: The Woman's Rights Movement in the United States*. Rev. ed. Cambridge: Belknap-Harvard University Press, 1959.

Friedman, Jean E., and William G. Shade, eds. *Our American Sisters: Women in American Life and Thought*. Boston: Allyn and Bacon, 1973.

Fuller, Margaret. *Women in the Nineteenth Century*. 1845. New York: Norton, 1971.

Gilman, Charlotte Perkins. *Women and Economics: A Study of the Economic Relation between Men and Women as a Factor in Social Evolution*. 1898. New York: Harper and Row, 1966.

"Is There Such a Thing as Sex?" *Nation* 8 (1969): 87–88.

Kraditor, Aileen S., ed. *Up from the Pedestal: Selected Writings in the History of American Feminism*. New York: Quadrangle, 1968.

Lerner, Gerda. *The Woman in American History*. Menlo Park, Calif.: Addison-Wesley, 1971.

Martineau, Harriet. *Society in America*, Vol. II. London: Saunders & Otley, 1837.

O'Neill, William L. *Everyone Was Brave: The Rise and Fall of Feminism in America*. Chicago: Quadrangle, 1969.

Parker, Theodore. "The Public Function of Woman," 1853. Rpt. in Theodore Parker, *Sins and Safeguards of Society*. Boston: American Unitarian Association, 1907–1913, Vol. IX: 178–206.

Parkman, Francis. "The Woman Question." *North American Review* 129 (1879): 304–8.

Rossi, Alice S., ed. *The Feminist Papers: From Adams to de Beauvoir*. New York: Bantam, 1973.

Smith, Page. *Daughters of the Promised Land: Women in American History*. Boston: Little, Brown, 1970.

Smith-Rosenberg, Carroll. "The Female World of Love and Ritual: Relations between Women in Nineteenth-Century America." In *The Signs Reader: Women, Gender and Scholarship*. Edited by Elizabeth Abel and Emily K. Abel. Chicago: University of Chicago Press, 1983, pp. 27–55.

Stanton, Theodore, and Harriet Stanton Blatch, eds. *Elizabeth Cady Stanton*. 2 vols. New York: Arno, 1969.

"The Woman Question Again." *North American Review* 130 (1880): 25–26.

Index

About the Author

ANN R. SHAPIRO is Associate Professor of English, State University of New York at Farmingdale. A specialist in nineteenth-century American women's literature, she is co-author of an *Introduction to a Country Doctor by Sarah Orne Jewett* and has written several articles published in *Moment*, *Reader*, and *Radical Teacher*.